MAGGA

MAKE AMERICA GREAT AND GOD ALIGNED

YASEVA

Contents

Contents

Unveiling A Grand And Profound Vision

In a world yearning for balance, progress, and harmony, Yaseva emerges as a luminary, a profound socio-spiritual and geopolitical strategist. His groundbreaking approach is rooted in the values of diversity, equity, and inclusion and champions the principles of unconditional love, peace, and joy, while addressing present civilization's critical intersection of humanity and the planet.

A Revolutionary Blueprint for Global Harmony

In an era marked by transformative leaders in the United States and beyond, Yaseva aligns with the aspirations of greatness, excellence, and nobility. This is a call to action for America and the world to ascend to higher ideals, demonstrating that true leadership is measured not by power alone but by the ability to uplift humanity and safeguard our planet.

Through innovative strategies and programs, even the armed forces are envisioned as instruments of global good, ushering in a revolution of unasked offerings. This movement creates unprecedented opportunities for human flourishing, igniting a wave of positive transformation across the globe.

A New Paradigm of Envisioned Leadership

Yaseva's strategies resonate deeply with the positive prophecies of God, envisioning a future where the glory of divine joy envelops the world as the waters cover the sea. Guided by the principle that the meek shall inherit the Earth—not the warmongers, but the compassionate, the just, and the wise—Yaseva is redefining what it means to lead with both heart and mind. The descendants of Abraham, likened to stars in the sky, illuminate this vision, offering guidance and hope to a world seeking renewal.

A Call to Action

This monumental work unveils powerful transformative strategies, offering a blueprint for a new era where the largest group in history, 'The Descendants of Abraham', possessing the spirit of love, peace, and joy on earth. Together, they forge a path toward a global renaissance, where every nation, every leader, and every individual contributes to the flourishing of humanity and the preservation of the planet.

With unyielding faith, bold innovation, and an unwavering commitment to God's vision, Yaseva's mission stands as a beacon of hope, inviting the world to join this extraordinary journey of renewal. This is not just a book; it is a clarion call to revolutionize our present and shape a future worthy of divine glory. "Expanding the Reign of Love, Peace, and Joy on Earth, as it is in Heaven."

The time to act is now. Let this be the dawn of a new age.

SECTION A - THE PULSE OF THE TIMES

CHAPTER 1

The Assassination of Hassan Nasrallah

In the shadowy world of Middle Eastern politics and military intelligence, few figures have been as elusive or enigmatic as Hassan Nasrallah, the leader of Hezbollah. For over two decades, Nasrallah symbolized resistance in Lebanon against both Israeli forces and Sunni militant groups like ISIS. He was revered by some and reviled by others, but his ability to remain hidden from Israeli and Western intelligence agencies was legendary. However, in a dramatic and deadly turn of events, the long hunt for Nasrallah ended in a precision strike filled with intrigue, subterfuge, and state-of-the-art military technology.

Nasrallah had been a ghost to his enemies for years. He rarely made public appearances, and when he did, they were typically through recorded messages, ensuring his whereabouts remained unknown. His movements were a closely guarded secret, often shifting from location to location, ensuring that he never stayed in one place for more than a night. Israeli intelligence, known for its prowess, had struggled to pin him down. Despite their claims of being able to strike him at will, the reality was that they had often been a step behind, missing key opportunities to eliminate him.

The Unfolding Plot

In mid-September, the pieces of the puzzle began to fall into place. According to sources, an Iranian mole, possibly working for a U.S. intelligence agency, provided the crucial information. The price? Likely tens of millions of dollars, paid for a tip that could shift the balance of power in the region. The mole revealed details of Nasrallah's movements, pinpointing a crucial moment when he would be inspecting a stockpile of newly arrived Iranian missiles at Hezbollah's underground complex in Dahiya, a neighborhood in southern Beirut.

The tip-off set in motion a series of events that culminated in one of the most devastating airstrikes in recent Lebanese history. Nasrallah was scheduled to inspect the advanced weaponry—missiles recently delivered by Iran—in an underground bunker. This visit, highly secretive and essential to Hezbollah's operational strength, was meant to be routine but turned into a deadly trap.

The Plan of Attack

At the same time, diplomatic efforts to broker peace between Lebanon and Israel were underway. French President Emmanuel Macron, along with the U.S., had been negotiating a ceasefire between the two nations. Israel, seemingly in agreement, put on a public face of cooperation. Meanwhile, in the shadows, plans for a lethal strike were meticulously crafted. The U.S. clandestinely provided tactical espionage support, but the French were totally in the dark.

On September 27th, as Israeli Prime Minister Benjamin Netanyahu prepared to address the UN General Assembly in New York, Israeli jets were being readied at Hatzerim Airbase. Netanyahu's aircraft, the "Wings of Zion," took off for New York, where he would speak about peace even as Israeli intelligence confirmed Nasrallah's location. During the flight, Netanyahu and his defense aides discussed the operation, knowing this might be their last chance to eliminate the Hezbollah leader.

Late on Friday evening, just before the Sabbath, 80 Israeli F-15 fighter jets took off from Hatzerim, laden with precision-guided bombs, including the infamous BLU-109 bunker busters. These bombs, weighing 2,000 pounds each and costing around $3 million apiece, are designed to penetrate underground complexes before detonating. Their mission was clear: obliterate Hezbollah's leadership and destroy the underground bunker housing Nasrallah and his commanders.

The Strike

As the jets approached Dahiya, Hezbollah's stronghold in southern Beirut, the neighborhood appeared quiet. The target was an unassuming six-story building topped with solar panels, but beneath the surface lay an intricate network of tunnels and bunkers. The jets released their deadly payload, raining destruction on the complex.

Within seconds, the ground shook as the bombs penetrated deep into the earth before detonating. The massive explosion created a crater 65 feet deep, leveling the building and collapsing the underground bunkers. Multiple secondary explosions followed as the Iranian missiles stored within the complex ignited, turning the night sky into a blazing inferno. Over 700 people were killed in the attack, including Nasrallah, his daughter, and several top Hezbollah commanders.

Observers reported that the bombs dropped in rapid succession, with one hitting every two seconds. The precision and power of the strike were overwhelming. Buildings within a wide radius were either destroyed or severely damaged. Four residential structures were leveled, and at least 300 people were initially reported dead. The Israeli government claimed that Nasrallah had intentionally built Hezbollah's headquarters beneath civilian buildings, making the strike both necessary and justified.

The Aftermath

The assassination of Hassan Nasrallah sent shockwaves through Lebanon and the wider Middle East. Hezbollah's leadership had been decapitated, and Israel had achieved what had seemed impossible for years. But the cost was immense. Civilians were among the casualties, and the damage to Beirut's infrastructure was catastrophic.

The Lebanese government condemned the attack, calling it an act of war. Hezbollah supporters mourned the loss of their leader, and Christian political allies of Hezbollah voiced their sorrow. One Christian leader, an MP in the Lebanese Parliament, described Nasrallah as "a symbol, a legend, whose resistance will continue." Former Lebanese President Michel Aoun, himself a Christian, praised Nasrallah for his dedication to Lebanon's independence and his resistance against foreign aggression.

A Legacy of Resistance

Despite his death, Hassan Nasrallah's legacy endures. He was a leader who skillfully balanced the interests of Lebanon's diverse religious groups while fiercely opposing Israel's expansionist ambitions. Under his command, Hezbollah had become not only a military force but also a political movement with a powerful presence in Lebanon's Parliament.

For Israel, the strike was a tactical victory, but it may also have sown the seeds of further conflict. Hezbollah's supporters vowed revenge, and the group's military wing remains a formidable force even without Nasrallah at its helm.

The intrigue and subterfuge that led to Nasrallah's assassination reveal the complex and dangerous nature of the conflict. It was not just a simple act of military precision but a carefully orchestrated plot involving spies, moles, and months of intelligence gathering. In the end, it took a combination of Israeli and American involvement.

AGGA! America Acted Ghastly Again.

This violent assassination, carried out by the Israeli Armed Forces under the leadership of Prime Minister Benjamin Netanyahu, would not have been possible without the support of the United States at multiple levels. Only months prior, the U.S. government had approved a $4.5 billion arms deal, one of the largest in its history, supplying advanced weaponry to Israel. Among these weapons were bunker-buster bombs, each costing around $3 million. This arms package played a significant role in facilitating the operation, though at the time of the assassination, public scrutiny largely focused on Israel as the primary perpetrator.

The involvement of the United States, while less overt, became apparent to many observers. Critics pointed out that the U.S. had provided the tools that enabled this act, causing widespread condemnation among Palestinians, Arab-Americans, and sympathizers worldwide. Many were horrified by the collateral damage and loss of innocent lives resulting from such actions.

The assassination and U.S. involvement further tarnished America's global image, with some labeling it a nation complicit in aggression and militaristic expansionism. The Arab-American community and other groups voiced outrage, and protests erupted in universities and public forums, denouncing the perceived role of the United States in supporting acts of violence.

Despite the backlash, the military-industrial complex—which benefited enormously from arms sales—remained unaffected, as share prices of defense contractors soared. Meanwhile, the U.S. government faced significant criticism, with its actions being seen as prioritizing profit over principles.

This incident added to growing perceptions that the United States, rather than embodying ideals of justice and peace, was increasingly viewed as a nation willing to support destructive acts for economic and political gain. It raised serious questions about the moral and ethical responsibilities of a global superpower.

CHAPTER 2

Angels Lamenting the Death of Hassan Nasrallah:

Angel Gabriel: Gabriel, the mighty archangel who had delivered prophecies to the forefathers of the Abrahamic faiths, stood at the forefront of the mourning hosts. His voice rang out, lamenting the great loss. "The heavens weep today, for Hassan Nasrallah, a leader not of evil but of balance and strength, has been taken by force. The descendants of Abraham—Christians, Muslims, Jews, and all others who share this sacred lineage—had their place disrupted by his untimely death. Nasrallah was a leader who understood the complexity of the Middle East, who navigated the tensions between Isaac, Ishmael, and their descendants. He brought peace where there was strife and held Lebanon together amidst these forces."

Angel Michael: Michael, the warrior angel, raised his sword in solemn salute, his lament, tinged with righteous anger. "This is not the defeat of a terrorist as some would claim, but the murder of a man who balanced the powers of Abraham's descendants—Christians, Muslims, and Druze—in a turbulent region. He stood against the forces of ISIS, the Sunni militants who sought to tear apart Lebanon. At the same time, he shielded his people from the Zionists of Israel, who sought to seize Lebanese lands in the name of territorial expansion. In him, we saw a leader of great military genius and political wisdom, a man who forged alliances with Christians and protected their rights even as the Western world spread lies of persecution."

Angel Uriel: Uriel, the angel of wisdom and foresight, stepped forward, his eyes filled with sorrow as he reflected on the geopolitical realities that Nasrallah had so deftly navigated. "Let no one forget that Israel, in its quest for a Zionist state, mirrors the very ambitions of those who call for an Islamic caliphate. Both seek dominion through force and destruction. Nasrallah, from the tender age of 32, led his people for three decades, balancing the interests of Muslims, Christians, and others. It is a deceitful lie, perpetuated by the Western media, that Nasrallah persecuted Christians. In truth, he gave them space to worship, and many Christian leaders wept for him after his assassination. This was a man who stood against expansionist movements, a clever military strategist who saw through the machinations of Israel and its claims of 'defense' to justify annexation."

Angel Raphael: Raphael, the angel of healing, spoke in a voice filled with both grief and condemnation. "How can one mourn the loss of such a man without recognizing the brutality of his death? The Zionist regime of Israel, under the guise of diplomacy, prepares for peace with one hand while striking down their enemies with the other. On the eve of the Sabbath, with the world watching, they launched an attack of unparalleled destruction, killing not only Nasrallah but also countless others. They fired on UN peacekeepers, attempting to drive them away from the Blue Line, so that they could move unopposed. Even now, UNIFIL nations—Italy, India, Indonesia, and others—plead with Israel to stop its aggression. And yet, it is clear: Israel seeks to clear the way for territorial expansion."

Angel Azrael: Azrael, the angel of death, had witnessed the moment when the skies darkened with Israeli fighter jets and the bunker-busting bombs fell on the complex where Nasrallah and others were gathered. "At that moment, a crater 65 feet deep was created, and with it, the lives of Nasrallah, his daughter, and key figures in the resistance were ended. They were not alone in death, for the Iranian missiles recently supplied exploded in a chain reaction, sealing the fate of hundreds more. And yet, in this moment of devastation, Nasrallah's legacy endures. The people of Lebanon have not lost hope. His legend will rise even as his body falls, and the resistance continues."

Angel Metatron: Metatron, the heavenly scribe, who chronicles all of human history, took note of the political deceit and manipulation surrounding Nasrallah's death. "While the world watched, Israeli Prime Minister Netanyahu showed the world a map at the United Nations, erasing Palestine and Gaza, claiming those lands for Israel. His intentions were clear—to colonize not only Palestine but also Lebanon. The hypocrisy is staggering. Israel, supported by the U.S., who provided billions in military aid, is expanding its territory, even as it decries Hezbollah as a terrorist organization. Yet Hezbollah fought ISIS, defeated al-Qaeda, and stood against the Zionist agenda. This truth must be recorded for all time: Hassan Nasrallah was not the terrorist they claimed. He was a leader of the resistance, protecting his people from destruction."

Angel Seraphiel: Seraphiel, leader of the seraphim, whose praise echoes across the heavens, concluded the angels' mourning with a call to divine mercy. "Let it be known that the actions of the Zionist regime are not hidden from the eyes of God. The use of deceit, hypocrisy, and violence to further their aims will not be rewarded. God, who sees the sincerity of hearts, will show mercy to the descendants of Abraham. And the prophecy shall be fulfilled: they will be as numerous as the stars in the sky, united in peace, not divided by war. For today, we mourn the loss of Nasrallah, but tomorrow, we will see the triumph of justice."

CHAPTER 3

The Great Prayer of Angels for God's Mercy

The Heavens Resound with Lamentation and Hope In the highest realms of heaven, where light and glory flow from the very presence of the Almighty, a great assembly of angels had gathered. Their wings, brilliant and iridescent, shimmered with divine light as they stood in solemn prayer. The air, usually alive with songs of praise and exultation, was heavy with grief, for the assassination of Hassan Nasrallah, the Hezbollah leader, had shaken the hearts of the angelic hosts. This was not merely the loss of a man; it was a blow that reverberated through the spiritual realm, echoing the sorrow and violence that plagued the Earth. The angels knew that their response had to be more than mourning—they had to plead for God's mercy upon the descendants of **Abraham** and upon all humanity.

Amidst the assembly, **Archangel Gabriel**, the great messenger of the Lord, stood tall, his wings shimmering with the golden light of wisdom and revelation. Gabriel, who had once brought prophecies to Earth's prophets, now raised his voice to heaven in a prayer that called upon the mercy of God. His words, as powerful as they were reverent, flowed like rivers of light through the vast expanse of the celestial realm.

"O Lord, Creator of the heavens and the Earth," Gabriel began, his voice resonating with authority, "we come before you to plead for your mercy upon the **descendants of Abraham**, your chosen servant. For you promised that through Abraham, all the nations of the world would be blessed. And now, as we witness the violence and strife among these descendants, we ask for your divine intervention."

The angels, their wings fluttering in soft agreement, listened intently as Gabriel's prayer continued. His voice grew stronger as he spoke of **Ishmael**, the firstborn of Abraham, whose descendants were scattered across the vast deserts of **Arabia.** "We pray for the sons of Ishmael, O Lord," Gabriel intoned. "Through Ishmael, you raised up twelve princes, and his descendants have multiplied into great nations. Wherever they are, O God, bring them together in peace. Let them walk in the spirit of discernment and wisdom, understanding the depth of your love, your mercy, and your call to **meekness**—for it is the meek who shall inherit the Earth."

The assembly of angels responded with a resounding **"Amen,"** their voices blending into a harmonious chorus that filled the heavens with the sound of divine reverence. Gabriel continued, his words flowing like streams of divine grace, "Grant them, O Lord, the ability to turn away from violence and strife. Let them inherit the Earth as you have promised through Yeshua, the Lord of unconditional love."

With a nod, **Archangel Michael**, the protector and defender of God's people, stepped forward. His powerful presence filled the celestial assembly with an air of authority, his gleaming sword raised high as he addressed the Almighty. "O God, we pray now for the descendants of Isaac, the son of your covenant, the son of Abraham's promise. From Isaac, you raised up Jacob, who became Israel, and from Jacob, the **twelve tribes** emerged, blessed and chosen by you to be a light unto the nations."

Michael's voice thundered across the heavens like the roar of a mighty storm. "We ask that you remember these twelve tribes, scattered across the Earth, O Lord. Wherever they may be, may your grace be upon them. Let them be reminded of the sacred responsibility you have placed upon them—to shine with your light, to lead the nations in justice, and to proclaim the truth of your covenant with Abraham."

The angels bowed their heads in agreement, their wings glowing with the reflection of Michael's prayer. His voice, though filled with power, softened as he continued, "Let their hearts be softened, O Lord. Let them turn away from division and strife, from hatred and war. Let them remember that they are brothers, all children of Abraham, and let them find peace in your mercy."

With Michael's prayer lingering in the air, **Angel Uriel**, the angel of divine wisdom and enlightenment, stepped forward. His face shone with the brilliance of a thousand suns, his wings pulsing with the light of understanding. "O Lord of infinite mercy," Uriel began, his voice calm and steady, "we now lift up to you the descendants of **Keturah,** Abraham's third wife. Her five sons, O Lord, have also been blessed by your promise, and their descendants have spread across the lands. Let your mercy flow upon them, wherever they may be."

Uriel's prayer was a song of wisdom, each word a note in the divine symphony of heaven. "We pray that they be grafted into the vine of Abraham's covenant, that they too may share in the blessings you promised to your faithful servant. Let them walk in your grace, O God, and let them find peace and unity with their brothers, the descendants of Ishmael and Isaac."

The angels responded with another harmonious **"Amen,"** their voices blending into a single note of agreement as Uriel's prayer filled the celestial skies. **Angel Raphael**, the healer, then stepped forward, his wings shimmering with the light of divine compassion. His voice, soft yet filled with power, rose as he began his prayer.

"O Lord, whose love knows no bounds, we now pray for those who have been grafted into the vine of Abraham through the work of **Yeshua** and the **Apostle Thomas**. We remember the work of Thomas, who brought your message of love to the distant lands of **India,** to the people of **South India**—the **Tamil** people—who embraced the way of love and established a faith rooted in the truth that God is love."

Raphael's voice grew in intensity as he continued, "We pray for the **Saivite** and **Vaishnavite** traditions, O Lord, those who worship in the names of life and love. Let your mercy be upon them. Open their hearts to see the divine love of Yeshua, who came to unite all people in your grace. Let them walk in the truth of your love, and let them recognize that they too are part of the great family of Abraham, bound by your covenant of love."

The angels responded with a deep and resounding "Amen," their voices filled with the light of hope. Raphael then turned his attention to the **Mahayana Buddhists** and Svetambara Jains, those who had embraced paths of compassion and service. "We pray now for the Mahayana Buddhists, O Lord," Raphael continued, his voice rich with compassion. "These souls who seek enlightenment through selfless service, who walk the path of the **Bodhisattva**, have long sought to bring peace to a troubled world. O God, let your mercy open their hearts to the fullness of your divine love. Let them see in Yeshua the ultimate example of the **suffering servant,** and let them be drawn closer to your light."

The angels whispered their agreement, their wings glowing softly as Raphael's prayer for the Mahayana Buddhists filled the heavens. He continued, "We also lift up to you the **Svetambara Jains,** those who are devoted to helping the blind, the disabled, and the vulnerable. O God, let your mercy shine upon them as they walk in their mission of compassion. Let them be united with your divine purpose, and let them find peace and fulfillment in the light of your love."

The angels joined together in a resounding **"Amen,"** their wings fluttering in approval as Raphael's prayer came to an end. Yet there was more to pray for, and so **Angel Azrael**, the keeper of souls, stepped forward. His voice, deep and resonant, filled the celestial court as he addressed the Lord.

"We remember the **Sikh people**, O Lord," Azrael began, his voice steady and solemn. "Guided by the teachings of **Guru Gobind Singh**, they have walked the path of devotion, seeking peace, justice, and unity in a world torn by division. Let your mercy be upon them, O Lord. Let them know that they, too, are part of the great inheritance of Abraham, and that your love binds them to this sacred lineage."

The angels responded with reverence, their voices echoing Azrael's solemn prayer. "Let them be reminded," Azrael continued, "that they are part of the divine promise made to Abraham. Let your grace flow through them, uniting them with all of your children in love and peace."

With Azrael's prayer still fresh in their hearts, the angels turned to **Angel Metatron**, the scribe of heaven. Metatron, ever the faithful recorder of divine events, stood tall as he began to speak, his voice calm and measured. "O God of mercy, we record these prayers in the **Book of Eternity,** that they may stand as a testament to your love for all the descendants of Abraham. Let it be known in heaven and on Earth that your mercy extends to all, that your covenant is for all, both genetic descendants and those who have been grafted into the vine through faith."

Metatron's quill moved swiftly, recording every word, every prayer, as he continued, "We inscribe the prayers for the **Jews, Christians, Muslims, Mahayana Buddhists, the Svetambara Jains, the Saivites, the Vaishnavites, and the Sikhs—the Eightfold Religions in the family of Abraham.** May they walk in peace, let them be united in love, and let your divine purpose be fulfilled through them."

The angels stood in awe as Metatron's prayer was inscribed in the heavenly record, knowing that these prayers would stand for all eternity. Finally, **Seraphiel,** the leader of the **seraphim,** raised his voice in a majestic cry. His words, like a flame, burned with the intensity of divine praise as he spoke.

"O God of hosts, we conclude this prayer with a plea for peace among all the descendants of Abraham and all those grafted into the vine of Abraham through

Yeshua. Let there be peace among these peoples, O Lord. Let the descendants of Abraham no longer fight one another but come together in love and unity, for they are bound by your promise, your covenant of grace."

The angels lifted their wings in unison, their voices rising together in one final, glorious song. **"O Lord of mercy, pour out your grace upon the Earth! Let the descendants of Abraham shine like stars in the heavens, united in love, peace, and justice."**

As their voices ascended to the throne of God, the angels stood in awe of the divine plan. They knew that the descendants of Abraham—genetic and spiritual—would one day be united in the eternal embrace of God's love, fulfilling the promise made to Abraham long ago. The heavens resounded with praise, for God's mercy had been called upon, and the angels awaited the day when peace would reign across the Earth, and the descendants of Abraham would walk together as one.

CHAPTER 4

The Nine-Fold Expansion of Abraham's Descendents

In the endless expanse of the heavenly realms, where light and glory intermingle with the very breath of God, a profound event was taking place. The angels, radiant in their splendor, had gathered once more for prayer and reflection, their luminous wings shimmering as they stood in perfect harmony, lifting their voices to the Divine. They were united in a common cause: to mourn, to praise, and to pray for God's mercy upon the Earth, particularly after the violent assassination of Hassan Nasrallah. But something unexpected was about to unfold, something that would reverberate through all of creation, from the highest heights of heaven to the farthest corners of Earth.

Archangel Michael, the greatest of warriors, a prince among angels, stood at the center of this vast assembly. His posture was upright and commanding, his wings unfurled, gleaming with the glory of one who had stood before the Almighty for eons. Yet as the angelic hosts sang their songs of lamentation and prayer, Michael's heart was stirred by a sudden and divine revelation. Like a flash of lightning from the throne of God, the memory of a sacred truth surged into his mind—a truth that would change the course of their prayers and ignite a celebration unlike any other.

In an instant, Michael's eyes blazed with divine understanding. His voice, like the rolling thunder of a thousand storms, broke through the symphony of angelic voices. **"Behold!"** Michael called out, his words echoing through the vaulted heavens, shaking the very foundations of the heavenly courts. **"We have forgotten something of monumental importance! We have overlooked a profound truth: the Yeshuans! The assembly of all those who have love-occupied hearts!"**

At the mention of this sacred group, the angelic hosts paused, their voices faltering as they turned their full attention to Michael's proclamation. The air, thick with anticipation, seemed to pulse with the divine energy that radiated from the archangel. **"Yes, the Yeshuans,"** Michael continued, his voice both fierce and compassionate. **"Those on Earth who follow the path of unconditional love, who walk in the footsteps of Yeshua, the Master of Love, are grafted into the Divine Vine of Abraham!"**

The revelation struck the angelic assembly with the force of divine truth. Gasps of astonishment rippled through the celestial hosts, their wings trembling as they absorbed the full meaning of Michael's words. **The Yeshuans—those who had chosen to follow the way of love, who lived by the teachings of Yeshua, the one who brought self-sacrificing love to Earth—were part of Abraham's lineage, part of the great covenant that God had made with His chosen servant.**

Before Yeshua, Michael explained, unconditional love had not been present on Earth in its purest form. But Yeshua, through his life and death, had established a new way, a path of love that transcended all boundaries, a love that would unite people of all faiths, nations, and origins. **"Anyone and everyone,"** Michael continued, his voice swelling with authority, **"who follows the path of love is following Yeshua, whether they know his name or not. And in doing so, they become part of the family of Abraham, grafted into the Divine Vine, bound to the sacred lineage of those who have received God's covenant."**

At this proclamation, the entire assembly of angels erupted into joyous acclamation. The sound was overwhelming, a symphony of celestial voices that rang through the endless expanse of heaven. **"Yes! Yes!"** they cried, their voices like the rushing of mighty waters. **"We had forgotten this glorious truth! The ninefold descendants of Abraham are now complete!"**

For a moment, all of heaven was filled with the radiant celebration of this new reality. The angelic hosts clapped their wings together, their laughter and praise rising like a great cloud of incense before the throne of God. They danced upon the clouds, their movements synchronized in perfect unity as they celebrated the inclusion of the Yeshuans into the Abrahamic fold. The joy was contagious, spreading like wildfire through the ranks of angels, from the highest seraphim to the humblest cherubim.

"The ninefold descendants of Abraham!" they chanted, their voices rising and falling in waves of exaltation. **"God's covenant is expanding! The family of Abraham grows ever larger!"** And as they praised, their voices reached the farthest corners of the universe, resounding through the stars and planets, declaring to all creation that God's promise was being fulfilled in ever-greater measure.

Amidst this celebration, Michael, still standing at the center of the assembly, raised his hand for silence. His voice, though gentle, carried the weight of divine authority as he addressed the angelic host once more. **"Brothers and sisters of heaven,"** he began, **"there is more to this story. Even as we speak, something monumental is happening on Earth. The Yeshuans, those who follow the path of love, are gathering in a global virtual conclave."**

At these words, the angels fell silent, their anticipation building as they leaned forward, eager to hear more. **"This conclave,"** Michael continued, **"is titled 'Yeshua the Panacea,' and it is happening now, in this very moment! The faithful are gathering from every corner of the Earth to declare that Yeshua—the Lord of Love—is the cure, the remedy, the holistic panacea for all the ailments of the world!"**

The angels were stunned. They exchanged astonished glances, their eyes wide with amazement. Only a few of the wisest and most connected angels had known of this sacred gathering, and even they had not fully grasped its significance. But now, at Michael's announcement, the magnitude of the event became clear.

In a swift and dramatic motion, Archangel Michael raised his hand once more, and with a single, decisive gesture, he plugged the entire angelic assembly into the unfolding conclave on Earth. In an instant, the angels were transported in spirit to witness the grand event—a convergence of hearts and souls from every nation, every tribe, and every language, all united by one common force: **the love of Yeshua.**

The angels gasped as they beheld the sight before them, of hundreds of Yeshuans, gathered across the globe, connected virtually, united in spirit. They were chanting, praying, singing praises to Yeshua—the Panacea for all of humanity's afflictions. **"Yeshua the Panacea!"** the faithful cried. **"Yeshua the healer! Yeshua the liberator!"**

The angels could feel the power of the conclave surging through the Earth. It was more than just a gathering—it was a spiritual movement, a cosmic alignment that had been set into motion by divine will. The angels, their hearts overflowing with joy, began to chant in unison with the Yeshuans, their voices echoing through both heaven and Earth.

"Yeshua the Panacea!" they sang, their voices resonating with the chorus of humanity below. **"The Magnificent Panacea! The cure for all that ails the world!"** Their wings beat in time with the rhythm of the conclave's prayers, creating a symphony of celestial harmony that intertwined with the earthly praise.

As the vision of the conclave unfolded before their eyes, Michael stood tall, his voice ringing out above the angelic choir. **"Let it be known across all of creation!"** he proclaimed, **"Yeshua is the Powerful Panacea! He is the cure for every ailment, the remedy for every pain, the liberator of all who are bound! Through his love, the world is healed. Through his sacrifice, the world is saved. He is the Panacea for every broken heart, for every shattered dream, for every soul held captive by darkness."**

The angels, enraptured by the vision, lifted their voices even higher. **"Yeshua the Panacea!"** they cried. **"He who sets the captives free! He who brings light to the darkness! He who binds up the brokenhearted and makes all things new!"** Their voices filled the heavens and the Earth, creating a chorus of praise so magnificent that it seemed to shake the very foundations of the universe.

As the angels continued to sing, Michael turned to the assembly once more, his eyes blazing with divine fire. **"Look!"** he said, pointing toward the Earth. **"See how the faithful are gathering! See how their love for Yeshua transcends all boundaries! They are being accelerated toward the Divine Light. They are being liberated from all that binds them, from all that keeps them in darkness, and they are being drawn ever closer to God."**

The angels beheld the Earth, their eyes wide with wonder. They could see the spiritual transformation that was taking place. Chains of despair were being broken, prisons of hatred were being torn down, and the light of Yeshua's love was spreading like wildfire, illuminating the darkest corners of the world.

"Yeshua the Panacea!" the angels sang once more, their voices now in perfect harmony with the earthly conclave. **"Yeshua the healer! Yeshua the liberator! Yeshua the savior of all!"**

And as they sang, the boundaries between heaven and Earth seemed to dissolve. The spiritual and the material, the celestial and the terrestrial, were united in one glorious moment of divine worship. The angels and the Yeshuans were as one, their voices rising together in praise of the one who had brought unconditional love to the world—the one who had fulfilled the ancient promise made to Abraham, the one who had grafted all people into the Divine Vine of God's covenant.

"Yeshua the Panacea!" the chorus echoed across the cosmos, resounding from the highest heaven to the deepest depths of the Earth. **"Yeshua the Master of Love!"** And in that moment, all of creation—both seen and unseen—was united in one glorious prayer, one magnificent song of praise, hope, and love. For Yeshua, the Panacea, had come. And through his love, all were being healed, all were being set free, and all were being drawn ever closer to the heart of God.

Thus, the heavens and the Earth stood in awe, their voices joined in perfect harmony, proclaiming the Majesty of Yeshua the Panacea, the one who heals, the one who saves, the one who liberates all of creation.

And the great conclave of Yeshua continued to unfold, as the angels watched in wonder, knowing that the fulfillment of God's promise was not only at hand—but had already begun.

The celebration of Abraham's expanded covenant reached new heights, with divine love flowing through all of creation.

SECTION B – CONNECTING WITH THE DESCENDANTS OF ABRAHAM

CHAPTER 5

Day One - The Global Virtual Conclave

The Global Virtual Conclave of the Yeshuans had reached an electrifying moment. The atmosphere was charged with a sense of divine urgency, as the mission of **Yeshua the Panacea** unfolded. The compère of the conclave, with a voice filled with authority and warmth, greeted the global audience—hundreds of viewers across continents, tuning in from bustling cities to towns and villages.

"We gather not just as a global audience but as a unified spirit, yearning for the transformation of this world through the joy of Yeshua. We are here to break boundaries, transcend differences, and celebrate the universal call of love, peace, joy, justice, compassion, and righteousness."

As he spoke, the heavens above were filled with a stirring restlessness. The angels, who had been observing the conclave, sensed a deeper, unspoken need for divine guidance. The angelic assembly, radiant with divine light, shifted in anticipation, their wings trembling with spiritual energy.

Suddenly, one of the angels, overcome by the urgency of the moment, burst into prayer. With wings spread wide and a voice that echoed like thunder, the angel cried out, **"Spirit of God, lead this mighty conclave of Yeshua! Guide these earthly proceedings so that they may truly transform the nations, particularly the Middle East, where the descendants of Abraham remain divided by ancient conflicts."**

The angel's plea carried a deep, resonant power, as the words flowed forth like a river of divine intent. **"O Lord of all creation, let the children of Ishmael, Isaac, and Keturah recognize that they are partakers of your eternal blessings to patriarch Abraham. Let them set aside their differences, embrace one another as kin, and walk in the love of Yeshua, which is the ultimate manifestation of your love on Earth."**

The entire angelic assembly responded with an overwhelming cry of **"Amen!"** Their voices rang through the celestial realm like a chorus of a thousand trumpets. Their wings shimmered with radiant colors—gold, silver, and fiery red—as they joined in a unified prayer for the descendants of Abraham.

At this moment, as if touched by a sudden inspiration from above, the compère raised his hand, calling for a moment of silence among the virtual participants. **"Let us take a moment,"** he said solemnly, **"to reflect on the unity that Yeshua calls us to. It is not merely a matter of politics or diplomacy—it is a spiritual union, a gathering of all peoples into the divine vine promised to Abraham."**

The silence was profound, as the participants across the globe joined in quiet contemplation. It was as if a divine stillness had descended upon the conclave, a pause in time where the hearts of humanity could be reset. In this moment of reflection, the angels above resumed their fervent prayer.

"Master of all," one angel continued, **"we ask that you bring a supernatural awakening among the leaders of the Middle East and the world. Open their hearts, inspire them, and move them towards peace, love, and reconciliation. Let the descendants of Abraham be like stars in the sky, shining together in unity, as was promised."**

Another angel, filled with compassion, stepped forward. With tears streaming down his radiant face, he pleaded, **"O Spirit of God, let this conclave ignite a flame of hope among all nations, especially in the lands where Abraham's descendants dwell—not in conflict, but in love."**

As the angelic prayers intensified, the conclave seemed to be lifted into a higher spiritual dimension. The participants, whether leaders, followers, or observers, felt a surge of inspiration and hope, as if the divine presence had truly descended upon them. The compère, sensing the spiritual energy of the moment, spoke again.

"This conclave is not just an event—it is a divine mandate," he proclaimed. **"It is a call to action for every Joyist, every believer in Yeshua, and every person who seeks to transform the world through love. We are here to fulfill the covenant of Abraham, bringing together all his descendants under the banner of unity and peace."**

The compère, moved by the angelic intervention and the palpable energy of the conclave, made an impassioned call to the global audience. **"We are the instruments of Yeshua, chosen to lead humanity into a new era. Let us embrace this opportunity to heal divisions, uplift the downtrodden, and establish a world where joy, peace, and prosperity prevail."**

With this call, the conclave reached its climactic moment. The angels above continued their intercession, their voices blending into a heavenly symphony that resonated across the spiritual and physical realms. Their prayers were filled with visions of unity—a time when all peoples, regardless of their origins, would gather under the divine covenant of love, fulfilling God's promise to Abraham.

The Convergence of Religions – The Gathering of Abraham's Descendants

The Global Virtual Conclave of the Yeshuans had reached the point where the compère, brimming with enthusiasm, addressed the global audience with a solemn tone as he invited the International Convenor, **Yaseva,** to deliver his address.

The compère began with a detailed introduction of Yaseva, highlighting his extraordinary role in bridging the world's major religions. **"Yaseva,"** he announced with pride, **"has been at the forefront of efforts to converge the spiritual aspirations of diverse faiths—be it Saivism, Vaishnavism, or any of the religions that have emerged from the Indian subcontinent. His mission is to unite humanity with the Great Wisdom, the Great Light, and the Eternal Spirit."**

Yaseva, a figure of immense spiritual influence, was emerging as a beacon of hope for seekers across religions—Christians, Muslims, Hindus, Buddhists, and more. His approach centered around a common message: that all religions are connected by the same fundamental desire—to seek God, to merge with the divine light, and to bring joy, love, and peace to Earth.

As Yaseva stepped onto the digital stage, his presence was both calming and electrifying. He began his address with a powerful opening statement: **"My brothers and sisters, we are gathered here not merely to discuss philosophical ideals but to respond to the most pressing call of our time—the call for unity among the descendants of Abraham, as God promised in ancient times. But first, we must address the ongoing strife in the Middle East, where the Zionist expansion continues to fuel violence."**

Yaseva's voice took on a tone of deep sorrow as he continued, **"The Zionists, driven by territorial ambition, have taken up arms to expand their borders, contrary to the will of God. The God we serve is not a god of war and destruction, but a God of dialogue, understanding, and reconciliation. He** desires that we find common ground and celebrate the essence of love, joy, and peace. Yet, the history of displacement, injustice, and relentless aggression has only deepened wounds. This is the reality that we must transform, and it is why this Global Virtual Conclave is dedicated to the descendants of Abraham."

Yaseva paused, allowing his words to sink in. The audience was silent, sensing the gravity of his message. **"The mission of this conclave,"** he continued, **"is to fulfill the covenant that God made with Abraham—that his descendants would be as numerous as the stars in the sky, shining brightly with divine light. It is time for us to turn this vision into reality, to make peace a living force in the Middle East, the heart of our world's spiritual heritage."**

In the heavens above, the angels watched intently, their hearts lifted by Yaseva's words. They exchanged hopeful glances, realizing that the prayers they had fervently offered were being answered in the most unexpected and spectacular way. One of the angels, his eyes glistening with tears of joy, turned to his companions and exclaimed, **"Behold, the Spirit of God has guided the leaders of this conclave! They are focusing on the very promise made to Abraham—a promise that all nations and all peoples shall be blessed through his lineage."**

The angels bowed their heads in reverence, humbled by God's divine orchestration. The same God who holds eternity in the palm of His hand had moved the hearts of human leaders to fulfill His ancient covenant. The angelic assembly broke into spontaneous praise, their voices blending into a majestic song of gratitude:

"Praise be to the God of Abraham, the God of wisdom, power, and mercy!"

Yaseva, feeling the overwhelming spiritual energy that seemed to fill the entire virtual space, spoke with renewed passion. **"Today,"** he declared, **"we are not just calling for peace; we are manifesting peace. The vision of Abraham's descendants coming together in unity is no longer a distant dream—it is a divine imperative. We must put aside differences of creed, nationality, and politics and embrace one another as brothers and sisters, united by the love of Yeshua, the manifested love of God."**

The digital screens filled with messages of support from participants across the world. Some were representatives of Christian communities in Europe, others were Muslim leaders from the Middle East, and still others were Hindu monks and Buddhist lamas from Asia, all resonating with Yaseva's call for unity.

"The recent assassinations of leaders in the region," Yaseva continued, **"while tragic, are symptomatic of a deeper spiritual struggle. These leaders, despite their militant means, have been responding to the historical wounds inflicted upon their people. The founding of Israel itself displaced over 7 million people, an act of injustice that continues to fuel resentment. Our mission must be to heal these wounds, not deepen them."**

He raised his hand and looked skyward, as if seeking divine guidance. **"O God,"** he prayed aloud, **"let this conclave be a turning point. Let it be the catalyst for a new era, where Jews, Christians, Muslims, and all descendants of Abraham find peace, respect, and mutual understanding. Let them recognize that they are not enemies but fellow heirs of Your promise."**

The angelic assembly, sensing the depth of Yaseva's plea, began to sing a celestial hymn—a hymn that echoed the ancient promise made to Abraham:

"You shall be the father of many nations; your descendants shall be as numerous as the stars in the heavens."

The virtual audience, inspired by both Yaseva's words and the invisible presence of the angels, felt a surge of hope. Some wept, overcome by the spiritual weight of the moment, while others raised their hands in affirmation, pledging to work towards the unity of Abraham's descendants.

As Yaseva concluded his speech, he made a solemn vow. **"This conclave will not be just another gathering of words; it will be a movement of action, guided by the spirit of God. We shall work towards building dialogue, understanding, and trust among the nations of the Middle East. We will encourage interfaith gatherings, support socio-civic initiatives, and establish programs that nurture the spiritual and physical well-being of Abraham's descendants."**

He spoke directly to the participants, his voice filled with hope. **"Each of you is a torchbearer of this mission. You are called to shine the light of Yeshua's love, to create pathways of peace where there has been division, and to**

nurture the seeds of unity that have been planted today.”

The angels above, witnessing the sincerity and commitment of those on Earth, felt a deep sense of fulfillment. One of the archangels, his wings glowing with divine radiance, spoke to the others, **“This is the moment we have long awaited. The promise made to Abraham is being honored, not just by words but by hearts transformed. The Spirit of God is moving among the leaders, guiding them to bring about the divine reconciliation of Abraham’s children.”**

In this holy moment, the conclave seemed to merge with the spiritual realm. The boundaries between Earth and heaven blurred, as divine and human wills aligned in a singular purpose—to fulfill the ancient covenant and to establish peace as the foundation of the Middle East.

As the session drew to a close, Yaseva gave one final charge to the global audience: **“Go forth, not as individuals of divided faiths, but as united descendants of Abraham, guided by the love of Yeshua. Let us make peace, establish justice, and shine as the stars in the sky—together.”**

The conclave ended with the roar of applause from the participants and the heavenly chorus of angels, singing the praises of God. The virtual gathering had become a global spiritual phenomenon, transcending the constraints of screens and borders, and leaving an indelible mark on the hearts of all who had witnessed it.

The chapter closed with a sense of divine triumph, as the angels declared in one voice:

“The time of unity is at hand! The descendants of Abraham shall gather, and the world shall know the love of God, manifest in Yeshua!”

CHAPTER 6

Abraham's Expanded Legacy

Yaseva reappeared on the digital screen, ready to deliver an address that promised to be both historic and transformative. The participants of the Global Virtual Conclave of the Yeshuans, a diverse audience spread across the globe, awaited his words with a sense of profound anticipation. Yaseva, a spiritual leader known for his wisdom and inclusivity, began with a tone that carried both excitement and reverence:

"Friends from every corner of the world, this is a momentous time in human history," Yaseva proclaimed. **"Today, we gather not only to honor Abraham's legacy but to redefine it. We have received a divine revelation that expands our understanding of Abraham's descendants. Traditionally, we have seen Abraham's children as primarily composed of the Jews, Muslims, and Christians—those who trace their faiths directly to him. However, God's revelation is greater and more inclusive than we ever imagined."**

The digital audience remained silent, sensing that something unprecedented was about to be unveiled. The angels above, ever-watchful, felt the stirring of divine purpose as Yaseva continued.

"We must understand the heart of God and His covenant with Abraham," Yaseva explained. **"God promised Abraham that his descendants would be as numerous as the stars in the sky and that all nations would be blessed through him. This promise was not limited by lineage, by mothers, or by human divisions. It was a promise to all offspring of Abraham, whether through Hagar, Sarah, or Keturah."**

Yaseva's words carried a sense of divine urgency. **"God shows no partiality. He does not distinguish between the sons of one wife and the sons of another. In ancient times, it was customary for men to have multiple wives and even concubines, a fact that God considered in His promise to Abraham."**

Tracing the Complex Spread of Abraham's Lineage

Yaseva then recounted the complex story of Abraham's lineage, adding both depth and dramatic emphasis:

1. **Hagar and Ishmael:"In a moment of deep anxiety, Sarah, doubting God's promise, offered her handmaiden Hagar to Abraham. Hagar bore Ishmael, Abraham's firstborn. Yet, as soon as Hagar conceived, Sarah's jealousy arose, leading to mistreatment that forced Hagar to flee into the wilderness. Despite the hardship, God reassured Hagar that Ishmael would also be blessed, promising that he would become the father of twelve princes."**
2. **Sarah and Isaac:"God fulfilled His promise to Sarah despite her initial disbelief. At the age of ninety, she bore Isaac, the child of promise. Isaac grew up amidst complex family dynamics, marked by conflict between him and Ishmael, but God's covenant continued through Isaac, as well."**
3. **Keturah and Her Sons:"After Sarah's death, Abraham married Keturah, who bore him six sons—Zimran, Jokshan, Medan, Midian, Ishbak, and Shuah. These sons spread Abraham's lineage further, extending his blessings into new lands and cultures."**

As Yaseva spoke, the global audience was captivated by the sheer expanse of Abraham's descendants. **"The descendants of Abraham are not just a single family but a global phenomenon that has reached every continent,"** Yaseva declared.

Ishmael's Descendants and Their Spread

The digital screen lit up with a map depicting the spread of the Ishmaelites in the Middle East. Yaseva's tone grew more solemn as he spoke about Ishmael's twelve sons, whose descendants spread across Arabia, North Africa, and parts of Asia:

- **Nebajoth (Nebaioth):** Inhabiting Saudi Arabia, Jordan, and Iraq.
- **Kedar:** Spread across the Middle East and North Africa.
- **Adbeel:** Settled in Oman, UAE, and India (Gujarat).
- **Mibsam:** Present in Qatar, Bahrain, and Eritrea.
- **Mishma:** Found in Yemen and Somalia.

- **Dumah:** Located in Saudi Arabia and Syria.
- **Massa:** Inhabiting Saudi Arabia and parts of Turkey.
- **Hadad:** Found in Saudi Arabia and Negev Desert.
- **Tema:** Spread across Saudi Arabia, Togo, and Benin.
- **Jetur:** Present in Saudi Arabia and Turkey.
- **Naphish:** Located in Saudi Arabia and Egypt.
- **Kedemah:** Settled in Saudi Arabia and Iraq.

"The twelve sons of Ishmael established tribes that greatly influenced Arab culture, spreading Abraham's legacy across the Arabian Peninsula, North Africa, and even reaching parts of Asia," Yaseva explained.

The Scattering of the Twelve Tribes of Israel

Yaseva transitioned to the dispersion of the Twelve Tribes of Israel, outlining how historical events spread them across the world:

- **Assyrian Exile:** The Assyrian conquest led to the displacement of the northern tribes of Israel, marking the beginning of the Lost Tribes.
- **Babylonian Exile:** The Babylonians captured Jerusalem, causing another wave of dispersion.
- **Roman Conquests and Diaspora:** The Roman Empire's invasion and the destruction of the Temple of Jerusalem in AD 70 scattered the tribes even further.

Yaseva highlighted on the screen how the Twelve Tribes of Israel are believed to be dispersed today:

- **Reuben:** Found in France (Normandy region), Scotland (Clan Reuben), and Eastern Europe (Russia, Poland, Ukraine).
- **Simeon:** Present in Spain, Portugal, Latin America, and North Africa.
- **Levi:** Dispersed among the Jewish diaspora, with populations in Israel, the United States, and Europe.
- **Judah:** Predominantly settled in Israel, but also present in New York City, Ethiopia, and across Europe.
- **Dan:** Inhabiting Denmark, Ireland (Tuatha Dé Danann), Wales, and New England.
- **Naphtali:** Found in Norway, Sweden, Finland, and the Midwest USA.

- **Gad:** Present in Germany, Austria, Switzerland, and Pennsylvania.
- **Asher:** Spread across England, Netherlands, Belgium, and New England.
- **Issachar:** Located in England, Wales, Ireland, and the Midwest USA.
- **Zebulun:** Found in the Netherlands, Belgium, Canada, and New England.
- **Joseph (Manasseh and Ephraim):** Present in the United Kingdom, USA, Canada, and Australia.
- **Benjamin:** Scattered in Germany, Poland, Russia, and New York City.

The Six Sons of Keturah

Yaseva continued by describing the six sons of Keturah, their descendants, and the regions they are believed to have settled:

- **Zimran:** Associated with the Zimrani tribe of Arabia, contributing to the region's nomadic traditions and trade routes.
- **Jokshan:** Linked to the Arabian tribe of Jokshan, whose sons Sheba and Dedan established notable tribes in Southern Arabia and Eastern Africa.
- **Medan:** Settled in parts of the Middle East, known for expertise in horse breeding and equestrian culture.
- **Midian:** Associated with the Midianites, significant in Biblical history and providing refuge to Moses after he fled Egypt.
- **Ishbak:** Related to the Ishbaki tribe in Arabia, known for agriculture and water conservation in arid regions.
- **Shuah:** Linked to the Shuahites, renowned for their wisdom and diplomacy, often sought as mediators in tribal conflicts.

"The children of Keturah, like those of Ishmael and Isaac, are integral to the fulfillment of God's promise to Abraham. While the sons of Isaac became the twelve tribes of Israel and the sons of Ishmael became powerful Arabian tribes, Keturah's descendants played their part in shaping the spiritual and cultural landscape of the Middle East," Yaseva emphasized.

The Call for Unity and Reconciliation

Yaseva's tone took on a prophetic urgency as he addressed the modern-day conflicts in the Middle East. **"The Zionist expansion, driven by territorial ambitions, has been a source of ongoing strife. But we must remember that the God of Abraham is not a God of conquest but a God of reconciliation.**

The time has come for all direct descendants of Abraham to set aside their differences and embrace one another as part of God's covenant."

The angels above, filled with divine anticipation, sang hymns of hope and unity. One angel, radiant with divine light, proclaimed, **"Let this message reach every heart and every nation. Let the descendants of Abraham know that they are brothers and sisters, called to a divine purpose."**

Yaseva made a powerful declaration: **"Today, this Global Virtual Conclave is not just a gathering of ideas—it is the beginning of a movement of unity. It is a call for Jews, Muslims, Christians, and others to come together as one family, united by the love of Yeshua."**

The audience was moved, with many shedding tears of hope and joy. Yaseva continued, **"Our mission is not just spiritual but also practical. We must establish interfaith Yeshuan fellowships, promote socio-civic entrepreneurship, and work towards addressing climate change, poverty, and health crises. This is the true fulfillment of Abraham's covenant—bringing peace, prosperity, and unity to the world."**

Conclusion: A New Covenant of Unity

As Yaseva concluded, the heavens resounded with a chorus of angelic voices, singing praises to God: **"Oh God of Abraham, let your children shine like stars in the sky, united in love and peace."**

The vision of Abraham's expanded legacy, embraced not only by those on Earth but by the angels in heaven, determined to turn this divine revelation into a living reality.

CHAPTER 7

The Hero of the descendants of Abraham

As the Global Virtual Conclave progressed into its most transformative phase, Yaseva prepared to present a key chapter of Abraham's descendants—**Yeshua the 'Hero of Heaven'**, the promised one from the lineage of Judah, born around 4 BC in Nazareth. With his arrival, the covenant of Abraham reached its most pivotal moment, bringing salvation to a world darkened by sin.

Yaseva's tone grew intense as he began:

"Yeshua the Messiah, known as the Lion of Judah, came as the fulfillment of God's promise to Abraham, Isaac, and Jacob. Born in the humble town of Nazareth, Yeshua's mission was not only to redeem Israel but to be a beacon of hope for all of humanity. His message was one of unconditional love, mercy, and divine grace—a mission that changed the course of human history."

Yeshua's Mission: A Divine Call

For three years, Yeshua walked among the people, performing miracles, teaching divine wisdom, and exemplifying the true nature of God's love. Through acts of compassion, he healed the sick, forgave sinners, and uplifted the downtrodden. Yaseva emphasized:

"Yeshua was not merely a prophet or teacher; he was the embodiment of divine love—God's begotten son sent to redeem the world from spiritual darkness. He brought a new understanding of God's promise to Abraham, teaching that all nations would be blessed through this divine covenant."

However, Yeshua's message was met with fierce resistance. The very people he sought to save, the Jews, rejected him. Betrayed and condemned, he was crucified in 30 AD, at the age of 33, in one of history's most tragic acts of rejection.

The Resurrection and Birth of a New Movement

After Yeshua's crucifixion came the resurrection, a defining moment that ignited a new spiritual movement. Yaseva described it with a sense of awe:

"The resurrection was not just a return from death; it was the triumph of light over darkness, the birth of the Holy Spirit among believers. This event set in motion the movement of the Yeshua-followers, who became the 'People of the Way.' They were filled with divine love and went about spreading Yeshua's message despite persecution."

The early followers, transformed by the Pentecost and the descent of the Holy Spirit, displayed radical love and sacrificial living. They shared their possessions, lived in communities, and forgave even their persecutors. Rome, the heart of the Pagan Empire, saw them as a threat to its dominance, as these believers defied authority with their spiritual freedom.

"They worshipped secretly," Yaseva continued, **"meeting in catacombs, using the fish symbol as a mark of identification. Despite persecution, they remained steadfast, preaching Yeshua's message to anyone who would listen."**

The Turning Point: Constantine and the Cross

In the early 4th century, the fate of Yeshua's followers changed dramatically with Emperor Constantine's vision of the cross. Yaseva provided a detailed recount:

"Legend says that on the eve of a crucial battle, Constantine had a vision of the cross in the sky, accompanied by the words, 'In this sign, conquer.' He embraced this sign, attributing his victory to Yeshua, although the cross was not the form of crucifixion that Yeshua endured; Yeshua was crucified on a single pole, referred to as a 'tree' by the Apostle Peter."

Despite this historical nuance, Constantine declared Christianity the official religion of the Roman Empire, ending centuries of persecution and giving rise to the Roman Catholic Church. As the state religion, Christianity spread rapidly, transforming from a persecuted movement to a global faith.

The Rise of a Priestly Class and the Spread of Christianity

With the newfound freedom came the formation of a priestly class, a development that diverged from Yeshua's teachings, which envisioned all believers as kings and priests in God's kingdom. As Roman society adapted to Christianity, many pagan practices were absorbed, giving rise to new traditions and symbols.

"Yet," Yaseva emphasized, **"this transformation did not hinder the essence of Yeshua's message. Christianity, in all its forms—Roman Catholicism, Protestantism, and even Pentecostalism—remained focused on spreading the message of love, grace, and salvation. House churches, congregations, and missions sprang up worldwide, igniting a spiritual revolution."**

The Three Major Abrahamic Religions

Yaseva then shifted focus to the three major Abrahamic religions—Judaism, Christianity, and Islam—as descendants of Abraham's covenant. He spoke with both reverence and hope:

1. **Judaism:"The Jewish faith, tracing its lineage to Isaac, continues to seek the coming of the Messiah. Despite differences, the Jews have been faithful to the covenant, awaiting the fulfillment of God's promise. They are part of Abraham's expanded legacy, united with others in the hope of the Messiah."**
2. **Christianity:"Established through Yeshua, Christianity fulfilled the promise of redemption and extended the covenant's blessings to all nations. Christianity's growth and impact globally are a testament to Yeshua's mission, bringing the light of divine love to the farthest corners of the Earth."**
3. **Islam:"Founded in the 8th century by Prophet Muhammad, Islam recognized Yeshua as a prophet and acknowledged many aspects of the Old Testament. Muhammad described himself as the last prophet, guiding millions of Muslims to a relationship with God through the Quran. With diverse branches like Sunnis, Shia, and Ahmadis, Islam has become one of the fastest-growing religions globally."**

A New Revelation: The Expanded Abrahamic Covenant

As Yaseva neared the end of his address, he introduced a new revelation:

"Historically, the descendants of Abraham have been identified as Jews, Christians, and Muslims. But today, God reveals a broader understanding of His covenant—one that includes not only these three but also the descendants of Ishmael, Keturah, and the newly acknowledged tribes of the East. We are entering an era where all of Abraham's children will be recognized under the covenant of blessing, each carrying the divine spark

within."

The angels in heaven marveled at this expanded revelation. One angel, with tears of joy, exclaimed, **"The covenant is truly universal! God's love has no boundaries, and Abraham's descendants are more numerous than ever imagined."**

Conclusion: A Call for Unity Among Abraham's Descendants

Yaseva closed his address with a powerful call for unity:

"As the descendants of Abraham, we must set aside our divisions. Whether we are Jews, Christians, Muslims, or even the lesser-known descendants of Keturah and Ishmael, we are all recipients of God's promise. This new revelation beckons us to a broader unity—one where peace, love, and reconciliation become the pillars of our shared heritage."

The chapter ended with the angels above breaking into a celestial chorus, celebrating this new era of unity. The global audience, deeply moved by Yaseva's words, pledged to work towards peace among all of Abraham's descendants, knowing that this was not just the fulfillment of an ancient promise but the dawn of a new covenant for all humanity.

CHAPTER 8

Thomas's Journey to India and the Emergence of New Faiths

The Global Virtual Conclave now turned to one of the most remarkable stories in the spread of Yeshua's message: **Apostle Thomas**, the disciple often remembered for his doubt. Yaseva appeared on screen, his expression filled with admiration for this determined apostle.

"Thomas, the one who doubted and needed to touch to believe," Yaseva began. **"His journey is the embodiment of spiritual transformation and resilience. After touching Yeshua's wounds and exclaiming 'My Lord and my God,' Thomas's faith became unshakeable. He carried the message of unconditional love beyond the borders of Israel, venturing into distant lands to sow the seeds of faith."**

Thomas's Adventurous Journey to India

While other apostles remained close to Jerusalem and the surrounding regions, Thomas's spirit led him eastward, far beyond the familiar lands. Driven by a divine impulse and perhaps through interactions with eastern visitors in Jerusalem, Thomas found his path leading to the ancient subcontinent of India, a region rich in spiritual diversity.

Yaseva continued, describing Apostle Thomas's arrival:

"In 52 AD, Thomas reached the ancient city of Taxila, now in present-day Pakistan. Taxila, a renowned center of learning, attracted scholars from across the world. The city was vibrant with intellectual discussions in philosophy, astronomy, and medicine. It was also home to Buddhist and Jain monks, who followed the teachings of Gautama Buddha and Mahavira, founders of their respective faiths some 500 years before Yeshua."

Preaching Unconditional Love to Ancient India

In this diverse spiritual landscape, Thomas introduced the concept of unconditional love—a message that resonated deeply among the Buddhists and Jains of Taxila. Yaseva elaborated on Thomas's challenge:

"The prevailing spiritual philosophies emphasized withdrawal from desires and extreme asceticism as means to transcend suffering. Buddha, of Tamil origin, taught that desire was the root of suffering, advocating for detachment from worldly things. Jainism, similarly, upheld non-violence and renunciation, with monks sweeping the ground before walking to avoid harming even the smallest creatures. But for Thomas, Yeshua's message was different: it was not about withdrawal but about engagement through love."

Thomas's words carried a radical promise: God's unconditional love was freely available, not earned through austerity but through sincere faith. As Thomas laid hands on people, they experienced the Holy Spirit, igniting a new wave of spirituality.

Transformation in Taxila: Birth of Mahayana Buddhism and Swetambara Jainism

The Buddhist monks, initially skeptical of Thomas's message, began to reconsider their teachings in light of Yeshua's love. Yaseva explained how this interaction led to a significant shift:

"In Taxila, a new sect of Buddhism began to emerge, later called Mahayana Buddhism—the 'Greater Vehicle.' Unlike the earlier Theravada Buddhism, which emphasized personal liberation, Mahayana embraced the concept of Bodhisattva, or the 'suffering servant,' reflecting Yeshua's mission of love. Mahayana Buddhists opened their eyes to the world's problems and sought to alleviate suffering through compassion."

Simultaneously, among the Jains, Thomas's message sparked the emergence of Swetambara Jainism. The Swetambara, meaning 'white-clad,' emphasized compassion and caring for the sick, poor, and grieving. The concept of non-violence expanded beyond mere physical harm to include spiritual compassion and selfless service.

Yaseva's eyes shone with passion as he described these transformations:

"These new faiths—Mahayana Buddhism and Swetambara Jainism—emerged as spiritual responses to the message of unconditional love. They embodied Yeshua's spirit, creating pathways to a deeper compassion that transcended the boundaries of religion."

Thomas's Mission in South India: The Land of the Tamils

After sowing the seeds of love in Taxila, Thomas's journey continued southward to the Malabar Coast (modern-day Kerala), a thriving hub of trade and culture. Yaseva recounted Thomas's arrival with vivid detail:

"Landing in Muziris, a bustling port city on the west coast of India, Thomas found himself in the heart of Tamil culture. The Tamil people were known for their rich spiritual traditions and openness to new ideas. The region was a melting pot of Arab, Chinese, and Mediterranean traders, contributing to a vibrant exchange of philosophies and goods."

Thomas, with his profound message of love, quickly gained followers among the Chera Tamil people, who spoke the ancient Tamil language. Yaseva described the impact:

"Thomas preached the message of Yeshua's love with a zeal that resonated deeply among the Tamils. The Ayyavazhi movement, an ancient Tamil spiritual tradition that emphasized oneness with God, found a kindred spirit in Thomas's teachings. His ministry led to the rise of the St. Thomas Christians, a group that remains strong to this day, upholding the traditions of Yeshua's love and peace."

Persecution, Persistence, and the Final Sacrifice

Despite the success of his mission, Thomas faced resistance from traditionalists and local authorities. His teachings of love challenged the existing social structures and religious hierarchies, making him a target for persecution. Yaseva's voice took on a somber tone as he described Thomas's martyrdom:

"In the city of Mylapore (present-day Chennai), Thomas was confronted by hostile priests and rulers. Refusing to renounce his faith, he was martyred by a spear thrust, a testament to his unwavering commitment to Yeshua's message. His final words were said to be a prayer for peace and love among all people."

The angels above, observing this recollection, were deeply moved. One angel, with tears of both sorrow and reverence, whispered, **"Thomas's journey was not just one of geography but of spiritual expansion, carrying Yeshua's message to the furthest reaches of the Earth."**

The Legacy of Thomas's Mission: Unity in Diversity

Yaseva concluded his discourse on Thomas by highlighting the apostle's enduring legacy:

"Thomas's mission in India brought about a profound transformation, not only in the lives of individuals but in the spiritual landscape of an entire region. The integration of Yeshua's love into Mahayana Buddhism, Swetambara Jainism, and St. Thomas Christianity shows the power of unconditional love to unite diverse faiths."

Yaseva emphasized that Thomas's journey is a reminder of Yeshua's global mission, one that transcends borders, cultures, and beliefs. **"The message of love is not confined to any one faith,"** he declared. **"It is the universal language of the divine, spoken through Yeshua and carried to the ends of the Earth by apostles like Thomas."**

The chapter closed with a heavenly chorus, as the angels sang praises for the courage and sacrifice of Thomas. The participants of the Global Virtual Conclave pledged to honor Thomas's legacy by promoting unity, compassion, and unconditional love among all of Abraham's descendants. They were reminded that the true measure of faith is not in doctrine alone but in the embrace of divine love, just as Thomas had shown.

"Thomas's mission in South India was not just the spread of a new faith, but the transformation of an ancient culture. The Tamil people embraced Yeshua's love and wove it into their spiritual fabric, creating a tradition that values universal love, compassion, and spiritual wisdom."

The virtual audience of the conclave was deeply moved by this account. The angels in heaven, too, were filled with joy and reverence for the Apostle Thomas's courage and perseverance. They praised God for the love that had blossomed in South India, a testament to the power of the Holy Spirit and the enduring message of Yeshua.

As the chapter closed, Yaseva reminded the participants that Thomas's mission is a call to all people, urging them to embrace the universal love of God that transcends cultural and religious boundaries. The Tamil people's spiritual journey, rooted in love, continues to inspire and guide the world toward a more compassionate and harmonious existence.

CHAPTER 9

The Ninth Fold of Abraham's Descendants - The Sikhs, the Yeshuans, and the Universal Reach

With the eightfold lineage of Abraham's descendants established, Yaseva announced the final and ninth fold in the Yeshuan Global Conclave, dedicated to exploring the spiritual lineage of Sikhism and the revolutionary formation of the Yeshuans—a group that embraces humanity's wider potential for unconditional love.

The Eighth Fold: Sikhism and Its Roots

The eighth fold of Abraham's descendants emerged through Sikhism, a faith founded in the Punjab region of South Asia in the early 16th century by Guru Nanak. This faith, deeply rooted in monism, equality, compassion, truth, and self-discipline, embodies many of the same divine principles Abraham's teachings stood for.

Founding Principles of Sikhism

1. **Monotheism (Ek Onkar):** Sikhs believe in one indivisible, eternal God, mirroring Abraham's monotheistic foundation.
2. **Equality (Manas ki Jat Sabhe Ek Hai):** Guru Nanak emphasized that all humans are equal, transcending caste, creed, and social status.
3. **Compassion (Daya):** Sikhs are taught to show compassion and kindness toward all living beings, reflecting Abraham's call for mercy.
4. **Truth (Sacch):** The pursuit of truth and honesty aligns with Abraham's moral teachings.
5. **Self-Discipline (Atam-Vinigraha):** Self-control and resistance to vices mirror the tenets of Abrahamic ethics.

Rituals and Spiritual Practices

Central to Sikhism are the Five Ks, symbols of faith for initiated Sikhs:

1. **Kesh (uncut hair):** Symbolizes holiness and strength.
2. **Kara (steel wristband):** Represents unity with God.
3. **Kanga (wooden comb):** Stands for cleanliness and order.
4. **Kacchera (cotton undergarments):** Reflects modesty and self-control.
5. **Kirpan (ceremonial sword):** Embodies the spirit of protecting righteousness.

These practices highlight the balance between spiritual devotion and social responsibility, concepts deeply resonant with Abrahamic traditions.

Sikh Scriptures and Legacy

The Guru Granth Sahib, the sacred scripture of Sikhism, is a collection of hymns from the first five Gurus and other saints, reflecting a devotion to God that transcends borders. Guru Gobind Singh, the 10th Guru, instituted the Khalsa, a spiritual and warrior community committed to protecting justice and righteousness.

Sikhism's emphasis on equality, devotion, and interfaith dialogue makes it a vital branch in the expanded lineage of Abraham's descendants. It draws inspiration from Islamic monotheism, Vaishnavite bhakti, and indigenous Punjabi traditions, making it a bridge between the Abrahamic faiths and the spiritual paths of South Asia.

The Ninth Fold: The Yeshuans - A New Dimension in Abraham's Lineage

As the ninth fold, Yaseva introduced the Yeshuans, a global spiritual movement dedicated to embracing universal love that transcends religious boundaries. The Yeshuans represent those who embody unconditional love but may not identify with any specific religious tradition, creating a new space within Abraham's expansive spiritual family.

Universal Embrace of Love

Yaseva elaborated, **"The Yeshuans are those who practice unconditional love regardless of religious affiliation. This platform addresses the spiritual hunger of those who seek God through love alone, a principle central to Abraham's covenant."**

The Yeshuans encompass a broad spectrum of spiritual seekers:

1. **Traditional Worshipers:** Indigenous practitioners of nature worship, ancestral rites, and local deities.
2. **Humanitarian Atheists:** Those who do not follow any religion but demonstrate profound love through humanitarian work.
3. **Philosophers and Thinkers:** People in various fields who embrace love as a guiding principle in life, even if their primary focus is science or reason.

The Mission of the Yeshuans: An Open Invitation

Yaseva declared, **"The Yeshuans represent the ninth fold that completes Abraham's expanded lineage. This fold is open to anyone and everyone whose heart is filled with love, for where love is present, so is God."**

The Yeshuans aim to:

1. Foster a spiritual community for those without formal religious affiliations but who practice love.
2. Create platforms for spiritual growth, leading individuals from a basic understanding of love to a deeper experience of joy, peace, and unity with the divine.
3. Embrace the teachings of Yeshua, focusing on love as the central tenet and offering a pathway for those who wish to deepen their spiritual journey.

The Global Impact of the Ninefold Abrahamic Lineage

With the Yeshuans completing the ninefold lineage of Abraham, Yaseva emphasized the holistic nature of this spiritual family. **"Abraham's descendants now shine like stars, illuminating the world with love, compassion, justice, and unity,"** he proclaimed.

This expanded perspective of Abraham's descendants achieves the following:

1. Breaks down barriers between religions, cultures, and nations.
2. Builds bridges of understanding and cooperation.
3. Unites communities under the umbrella of unconditional love.

Moving Forward: The Role of Interfaith Initiatives

To solidify this vision, Yaseva called for various interfaith and community-building initiatives:

1. **Interfaith Dialogues:** Host conferences, workshops, and seminars that encourage interfaith dialogue, panel discussions, and cultural exchanges.
2. **Artistic and Educational Programs:** Organize art exhibitions, music festivals, and educational initiatives promoting the diversity of Abrahamic heritage.
3. **Community Service Projects:** Launch social service initiatives such as food banks, healthcare services, and disaster relief efforts.

These initiatives will create a global platform for the descendants of Abraham to unite, regardless of religious or cultural background, under the principles of unconditional love.

The Legacy of Abraham and the Call for Unity

Yaseva concluded by leading the participants in an interfaith prayer, invoking the spirit of unity:

"May the divine light within each of us guide us toward love and compassion, breaking down barriers and illuminating our shared humanity. May we strive to honor the diversity of the Abrahamic family, promoting understanding, cooperation, and peace."

Participants across the world recited the Abrahamic Family Pledge, affirm ing their commitment to the principles of unity, love, and mutual respect:

"I pledge to respect and honor the diversity of the Abrahamic family, strive for understanding and cooperation, and promote peace and unity for a better world."

The Culmination of the Conclave

As the Yeshuan Virtual Conclave concluded this momentous session, the participants felt the power of interfaith collaboration and the possibility of a new world order—one shaped by **love, unity, and peace, fulfilling God's promise to**

Abraham: "Your descendants will be as numerous as the stars in the sky."

The Yeshuans, representing the ninth fold of Abraham's descendants, stood ready to expand the message of love and joy to all corners of the earth, creating a spiritual renaissance that would transform lives, societies, and the world.

CHAPTER 10

The Grand Unveiling of the Abrahamic Unity

After Yaseva's profound exposition of the **Ninefold Descendants of Abraham**, the virtual gathering was enveloped in silence, followed by a swell of awe and reflection. The magnitude of the moment was tangible, as if the revelation itself had descended into the hearts of each listener, awakening a deep, spiritual interconnectedness rooted in the timeless promise given to Abraham.

An Unbroken Chain of Blessings

The concept of the **Abrahamic Covenant as a Divine Vine**, from which all nine branches drew their spiritual nourishment, felt like a long-lost truth reclaimed. Each participant felt as if they were a leaf on this magnificent vine, receiving life directly from the sacred roots of Abraham's promise. This was more than theology; it was a visceral experience of divine oneness that sparked spontaneous applause, chants, and jubilant cheers. The digital screen flickered with messages of joy, as people from diverse lands celebrated this moment of unity.

Manjula Devaraj Takes the Stage

The screen glowed brighter as a new figure emerged: **Manjula Dev**, the energetic and dynamic spokesperson for the Yeshuan community. Dressed in an elegant robe adorned with symbols of unity, she exuded both grace and strength. The anticipation was palpable as Manjula stepped forward, her voice a beacon of authority:

"Greetings, my dear brothers and sisters of the Abrahamic family! Today, we stand at the crossroads of a new dawn. We are not just individuals; we are living embodiments of Abraham's promise, shining like stars to illuminate the world with love, compassion, moral integrity, justice, selflessness, and altruism!"

Her words carried an almost musical cadence, weaving together inspiration and conviction. The virtual audience responded with nods, smiles, and gestures of encouragement.

Celebrating the Power of Unity

Manjula continued, her voice filled with enthusiasm and urgency:

"Let us break down the barriers that divide us, build bridges that connect us, and unite communities that have been separated for too long. This is our mission! We must embody the beauty of diversity within the Abrahamic family and contribute to a brighter future where love conquers fear, unity overcomes division, and peace prevails, ushering in an era of Divine Joy."

The energy in the virtual space intensified, and Manjula's face glowed with the power of her words:

"We are all branches of the same tree, nourished by the same divine sap, rooted in the blessings of Abraham. The unity in diversity that we exhibit here today is not just symbolic—it is the highest form of divine manifestation."

Invoking the Words of Martin Luther King Jr.

Her voice became solemn as she invoked a timeless quote from Martin Luther King Jr.:

"Love is the only force capable of transforming an enemy into a friend."

Manjula's eyes shone with conviction as she reached out, as if embracing each participant through the screen:

"This is our call—to transform animosity into friendship, fear into trust, and division into unity."

The digital crowd felt the weight of her words, and many appeared visibly moved, with tears in their eyes and hearts filled with renewed purpose.

The Abrahamic Family Pledge

With a sense of ceremony, Manjula announced:

"Let us now recite together the Abrahamic Family Pledge."

A bold text appeared on the screen, and Manjula led the recitation, her voice strong and clear:

"I pledge to respect and honor the diversity of the Abrahamic family, to strive for understanding and cooperation, and to promote peace and unity by all means."

The participants recited the pledge in unison, their voices merging across borders, cultures, and languages. The recitation echoed like a mighty anthem—a declaration of a shared destiny.

A Moment of Meditation

With a gentle tone, Manjula called for a moment of meditation:

"Close your eyes, dear family, and contemplate the divine light within you. This light guides us on the path of love and compassion, uniting us in our diversity and illuminating our shared humanity."

For a full minute, there was absolute silence, as participants across the globe closed their eyes and entered into a sacred moment of introspection. It was a shared stillness that transcended space and time.

A Vision of Global Togetherness

Breaking the silence with renewed vigor, Manjula's voice resonated with excitement:

"Brothers and sisters, let us carry forward this vision of global togetherness. No matter where we live, no matter our backgrounds, we are bound by the same covenant."

She outlined a bold vision for the future:

- **Art Exhibitions:** Celebrating Abrahamic heritage through painting, sculpture, and photography that depict shared narratives.
- **Music Festivals and Concerts:** Bringing together songs and hymns from all ninefold descendants to foster a spirit of interfaith celebration.
- **Documentary Films:** Producing powerful films that tell stories of interconnectedness, revealing the common threads within each tradition.
- **Exchange Programs:** Facilitating cultural exchanges, where members of the Abrahamic family visit one another, deepening bonds through face-to-face

interactions.

- **Homestay Tourism:** Promoting homestay tourism, where descendants of Abraham host each other, experiencing each other's cultures personally.

Her ideas were not mere dreams; they were actionable plans aimed at transforming the global landscape of interfaith unity. The crowd responded with enthusiastic applause, filled with a sense of possibility and purpose.

A Call for Action

With a radiant smile, she issued a call to action:

"Now, it is up to us to take this message forward. Let us each become ambassadors of Abraham's promise—agents of peace, unity, and love. We have the tools, we have the connections, and we have the vision. It is time to act."

As she raised her hand in a gesture of blessing, she led the audience in a final prayer:

"May the blessings of Abraham flow abundantly among us, nurturing seeds of love, compassion, and peace. May we be the light in the darkness, the joy in the sorrow, and the unity amidst division."

The Theme Song of the Abrahamic Covenant

As Manjula concluded her speech, the theme song of the Abrahamic Covenant began to play. It was a melodious, uplifting tune that spoke of unity, love, and hope. The virtual audience sang along, their voices merging into a chorus of harmony and joy. The lyrics were simple but powerful, echoing the essence of the ninefold blessings:

We are branches of one tree, united by love.
We shine like stars, guided from above.
Together we stand, divided no more.
Peace is our banner, and love is our core.

The song filled the digital space, transcending physical borders, and resonating with hearts across continents.

A Vision for the Future

As the music faded, Manjula took a deep bow, her face glowing with gratitude:

"Thank you, dear family of Abraham, for this unforgettable moment. We have begun a journey that will reshape the world. Let us go forth, guided by love, inspired by peace, and united by our shared covenant."

The participants rose to their feet—some with tears of joy, others with arms raised in unity. There was clapping, chanting, and a shared sense of destiny. The energy was overwhelming, and the collective spirit was almost tangible.

The virtual conclave ended, but its impact had only just begun. The spirit of Abraham's covenant was now alive in each heart, carried by those who had witnessed this transformative event. It was a living promise, ready to manifest in actions that would reshape nations, mend broken relationships, and bring about an era of peace, unity, and **Divine Joy**.

SECTION C – HEALING THE DESCENDENTS OF ABRAHAM

CHAPTER 11

Day Two –Global Virtual Conclave

The second day of the **Global Virtual Conclave of the Yeshuans** unfolded with an atmosphere charged with hope, anticipation, and deep reflection. The central theme of the day was **healing the descendants of Abraham**, a crucial step in addressing the historical wounds that have divided the world.

The Prelude to a New Dawn

The dawn of the second day arrived like the prelude to an epic tale. Though the assembly was virtual, it felt tangible, as if millions of souls had gathered in one immense space—a **digital coliseum**, not filled with battle cries, but with anticipation and hope. Every attendee, whether at a screen in a quiet room, a bustling office, or outdoors, felt the electricity in the air. The conclave was alive, not just another conference, but a **movement carrying centuries of yearning, faith, and unfulfilled promises**.

The Expansion of the Covenant

The events of the previous day had set an ambitious tone, with **Yaseva delivering a transformative exposition** on the **Ninefold Descendants of Abraham**. This was not a mere theoretical expansion but a **spiritual revelation**. Yaseva recast Abrahamic descent, broadening it from traditional bloodlines to encompass a **universal kinship**. It was a vision that stretched the ancient Covenant beyond conventional boundaries, touching Jews, Christians, Muslims, and all seekers of **truth, justice, and spiritual renewal**.

Yaseva spoke with the fervor of a prophet and the meticulous detail of a scholar, illustrating how the descendants of Abraham could be found in every corner of the Earth, **as numerous as the stars in the sky**, fulfilling God's promise.

A Living Force

Manjula Devaraj, who followed Yaseva, brought a different yet equally powerful energy. She celebrated the **ancient Covenant** as a **living force**, not a relic of the past but a guiding light for humanity through the darkness of the modern era. Her voice resonated with warmth and hope as she envisioned a future where all could find a sense of belonging under God's promise.

Her words ignited a collective enthusiasm, aligning attendees' hearts with a singular purpose, as if the ancient Covenant itself were breathing new life into the conclave.

A Call to Action

As the new day began, the **compere** returned to the virtual podium, balancing solemnity and anticipation:

"We have laid the foundation, but now, the work truly begins. Today, we move forward, not just in thought, but in action."

He paused, allowing his words to echo through the virtual space, before introducing the next speaker with enthusiasm:
"And now, I have the immense privilege of introducing John Romeo—a movie-maker and the media head of the Yeshuans."

John Romeo Takes the Stage

The digital screen came alive with John Romeo's image. He embodied **youthful energy and zeal**, a striking contrast to the weighty themes discussed. His passion was palpable, and his charisma instantly captivated the audience.

"Greetings, descendants of Abraham!" he began. **"We have gathered here from across the world, bound not only by our shared spiritual heritage but by our collective desire to create a new path forward."**

Shifting to a tone of deep contemplation, he continued:
"Yesterday, we laid out the broader framework of the Ninefold Descendants. It was a profound moment of realization. But today, we must move beyond understanding—it is time for action. The Covenant of Abraham is not a mere historical promise; it is a living, breathing mission that calls us to respond to the realities of our present time."

Confronting the Harsh Realities

Romeo's words hung in the virtual air, heavy with urgency:
"As we gather here in peace, we must remember that, in many parts of the world, especially in the Middle East—the very heart of Abraham's

legacy—people are facing violence and oppression. Gunfire punctuates the air, homes crumble under the weight of conflict, and lives are shattered. Innocence is a casualty, and the seams that bind the descendants of Abraham are torn apart. It's a cauldron of turmoil, erupting like a relentless volcano, leaving in its wake despair, division, and devastation."

The silence that followed was profound, filled with the collective grief of the attendees. Sensing the gravity of the moment, Romeo paused briefly before resuming with even greater intensity.

The Healing Process

"Today's session," he announced, "is not just about discussion. We will engage in Playback Theater—a powerful tool to relive history's pains, confront present truths, and envision a healed future. This is not mere storytelling; it is about feeling the pulse of our shared history, understanding the triumphs and the tragedies that have shaped the descendants of Abraham."

Romeo's voice rose with a sense of righteous zeal:
"We must heal the wounds that have festered for generations—the whirlpool of conflict that draws people into its dark, destructive depths. This vortex must not simply be confronted; it must be transformed. We must fill it anew with the spirit of dignity, justice, compassion, and elevated consciousness. It is not enough to hope for change; we must become the change."

A Shared Destiny

After a long and deliberate pause, Romeo spoke softly but with penetrating conviction:
"The healing of the descendants of Abraham is not just a task; it is a destiny that we are called to fulfill. And this destiny requires not only dialogue but a deeper spiritual awakening—a recognition of our shared humanity, our shared pain, and our shared hope."

Behind him, the screen illuminated with the day's focal point:
"The Healing of the Descendants of Abraham."

The words blazed across the screen in bold, golden letters, symbolizing the dawn of a new era. The attendees were enraptured, sensing not just a message but a **mandate** to heal and unite.

The Light Shines On

Romeo stood in silence, allowing the moment to resonate. Finally, he concluded: **"This is our calling. To heal not just the divisions among Abraham's descendants, but the divisions within ourselves. For in healing these inner fractures, we can create the conditions for global reconciliation, and in doing so, fulfill the promise of the Covenant—a promise not only for Abraham's descendants but for all humanity."**

As the screen dimmed, the impact of his words lingered. The second day of the conclave had not merely continued the journey; it had deepened it, laying the foundation for a movement that could reshape history. The conclave's light shone brighter than ever, heralding the beginning of a global movement for healing, justice, and the rebirth of a shared destiny.

CHAPTER 12

Playback Theatre"The Siege of Jerusalem: Faith in the Midst of Flames"

The Siege of Jerusalem in 1099 was a key event during the First Crusade, launched by European Christians to reclaim the Holy Land. It was a time of intense religious fervor and brutal violence.

Arrival at Jerusalem (June 1099)

After a harsh journey through Anatolia and the Levant, **12,000 Crusaders reached Jerusalem in early June.** The city, under Fatimid control, was defended by a small but determined Muslim garrison. Despite severe shortages, the Crusaders laid siege.

The stage is dim, and the spotlight focuses on **Leila**, a young Muslim woman in Jerusalem during the siege of 1099. Her face is solemn, her posture resilient, yet weighed down by grief. She steps forward, embodying the voice of the survivors, narrating the siege through her eyes alone.

Leila's Voice: Faith Amid Chaos

Leila's voice, burdened with grief, emerges like a lament for a world torn apart:

"I am Leila, a daughter of Jerusalem. They came in the name of God, yet what they brought was terror, loss, and a desperate struggle for survival. We faced not just an army, but the very darkness of humanity—masked as faith. They claimed to be saviors, yet what they left was ruin, a city bathed in blood instead of mercy."

Leila's words echo the haunting memory of the night before the invasion, when she stood beside her brother Yusuf, both of them clinging to hope as war drums beat ominously in the distance.

"Stay close to me, Yusuf," she had whispered with protective urgency. **"We must keep faith that Allah will protect us."** Yet beneath her firm words, her own heart trembled. Outside the city walls, the Crusaders' prayers rose—prayers that called for victory, for the 'cleansing' of the very people who had called this city home for generations. The soldiers on their own walls prepared for battle, but the doubts in their eyes betrayed the heaviness in their hearts. How could one speak of faith when facing such darkness?

The Storm Breaks: Chaos and Destruction

When the storm finally broke, it came with a fury that defied description. **The walls crumbled like the last vestiges of hope, and the Crusaders flooded the streets with a ferocity that seemed to defy all humanity.**

"Stay close, Yusuf!" Leila had shouted, pulling him through frantic crowds, the chaos around them threatening to separate them at every turn. She remembered Ahmed, a brave soul who stood his ground to buy them precious moments.

"Run, Leila! I'll hold them back," he had cried. But not even his courage could halt the flood of violence that swept through their beloved streets. **The city became a living nightmare—homes set ablaze, bodies strewn lifeless, and prayers drowned by screams of despair.**

Leila's heart cried out: **Where was mercy? Where was God?** It felt as if even the heavens had turned away.

In the Aftermath: A Fragile Hope

In the aftermath of conquest, Leila found herself among the few survivors, huddled in the ruins of a mosque. Exhausted and defeated, she held Yusuf close, whispering through tears:

"We have lost our home, but not our faith. We will rebuild, Inshallah."

But even those words felt fragile, empty. Ahmed, wounded and weary, looked at her with haunted eyes.

"Is this how God's will is fulfilled?" he asked, his voice filled with bitter disbelief. **"With blood instead of mercy?"**

Leila had no answer; her own heart was filled with the same despair, the same unanswerable questions.

Acts of Humanity Amid Despair

Yet even in the depths of suffering, **Leila witnessed moments of compassion—small acts of humanity that defied the brutality of war.** Despite their losses, they tended to the wounded, including those who had come to conquer them.

"We are all human," Leila had said to them, her voice filled with a weary wisdom. **"No matter which God we pray to."**

One day, Father Thomas, a Crusader priest, approached her with an offering of bread. His eyes were heavy with remorse.

"I cannot undo the wrong," he confessed, **"but I wish to help."** Leila accepted, not just the bread, but the gesture—a flicker of humanity amidst the ashes.

A Fragile Step Toward Peace

As months passed, the survivors of both sides began to make tentative efforts to coexist. They gathered not as enemies, but as people who had lost too much.

"We have lost much," Leila told them, her voice still carrying the weight of pain, **"but we can prevent further loss."**

It was not an easy dialogue, and distrust lingered, but it was a start—a fragile step toward peace in a city that had known only war. Ahmed's words echoed in her mind:

"Our spirit endures. Can we not rebuild—not as conquerors or the conquered, but as neighbors?"

Planting the Olive Tree: A Symbol of Renewal

Leila's thoughts turned to a simple act of reconciliation—one that symbolized a hope she dared to nurture. **In the heart of Jerusalem, she knelt to plant an olive sapling, a symbol of peace and renewal.** It was a small gesture, but it carried the weight of countless dreams.

"The Crusades brought unspeakable violence," she reflected, **"but even in the darkest times, there were moments of humanity that survived."**

Her voice, filled with both sorrow and hope, spoke of a truth that transcended the bloodshed:

"This is not just a story of conquest; it is also a story of hope. For even amidst the ruins, we found the courage to forgive, to rebuild, and to dream of peace once more."

Leila's Final Plea: Faith as a Bridge

Leila's final words carry the wisdom of loss and the resilience of faith:

"May this story remind us that faith should be a bridge, not a weapon, and that in the ashes of the past, we can still find seeds of reconciliation."

Her plea is not only for Jerusalem, but for all who seek to rise from the devastation of war, to rebuild not just walls, but bridges of understanding. And as she stands there, her story becomes more than just a tale of survival—it becomes a testament to the enduring strength of the human spirit and the hope that one day, peace will prevail over hatred.

Conclusion

"I am Leila, and my story is one of enduring strength. The siege of 1099 was marked by cruelty committed in the name of faith. For us, it was the darkest of days, but our faith remained unbroken. Small acts of mercy reminded us that true faith is about compassion, not conquest.

Amid the ruins, I saw the will to survive and the beginnings of reconciliation. The olive tree we planted is a testament to our enduring spirit and hope for peace. Jerusalem remains a city scarred, but not defeated. It is up to us to turn swords into words and hate into understanding. We are not vanquished. We are Jerusalem, and we will endure."

CHAPTER 13

Playback Theatre – "The Conquest of Constantinople: Echoes of Faith and Loss"

Introduction: The Siege and Fall of Constantinople (1453)
In April 1453, Sultan Mehmed II besieged Constantinople with a massive army and advanced cannons. Emperor Constantine XI and the outnumbered Byzantines resisted bravely, but on May 29, 1453, after 53 days, the city fell, marking the end of the Byzantine Empire and a monumental shift in regional power.

The stage is dark, except for a solitary light illuminating Maria, a Byzantine Christian woman. Her expression is weary, her eyes filled with unshed tears. She speaks slowly, each word laced with the sorrow of a lost city and a lost way of life.

Maria's voice, heavy with grief, emerges like the mournful echo of a vanished world:
"I am Maria, and I lived through the fall of Constantinople. It was not merely a conquest; it was the end of a world, a dream, and a faith that had sustained us for generations. It felt as if the very soul of our city was being torn away, brick by brick, and with it, everything we held dear. The walls that had once been our shield became the boundary of our despair."

Maria's eyes reflect the haunting memories of that fateful night when the towering walls of Constantinople stood against an impending doom.
"Father," she had asked with a flicker of hope, *"the walls have protected us before. Surely, they will again."*
But her father's reply was heavy with resignation:
"The walls have stood for centuries, Maria, but now, I fear the tide is against us."

His words echoed like a dark prophecy she could not bear to believe. Elder Michael, the city's spiritual guide, had urged everyone to hold onto faith, to find courage in the Cross. Yet, even his voice trembled under the crushing weight of impending tragedy.

The Final Assault and Loss

As the Ottoman soldiers gathered for the final assault, Maria imagined the inner turmoil of Ibrahim, one of their own.
"We take the city tomorrow," he might have confided to a comrade, *"but is this victory, or sorrow?"*

On the other side of the walls, Maria and her people clung to prayers, even as the ominous sound of siege engines grew louder. She asked herself again and again: **How could this be God's will? How could He allow His own city, His own people, to be torn apart?**

When the walls finally crumbled, the proud gates fell, and the defenders were overwhelmed. Maria clutched her mother's rosary, the beads growing heavier with every prayer that went unanswered. The breach of the walls brought chaos—another blow to hearts already battered by fear.

In the sanctuary of Hagia Sophia, Elder Michael gathered the people for one last stand of faith.
"Even if the walls fall, our faith must not waver," he implored.

But the Islamic call to prayer soon rose above their laments, slicing through the air like a knife, a stark symbol of the city's transformation. **What was once theirs was now filled with a foreign sound, and it was this piercing reality that marked the depth of their loss.**

Moments of Humanity Amid Devastation

The city's transformation was swift and merciless. Hagia Sophia, their sacred heart, was no longer theirs. The familiar streets turned alien as conquerors filled the once-vibrant spaces.

But amidst this devastation, unexpected moments emerged. One day, near the steps of Hagia Sophia, Maria was approached by a Muslim woman named Fatima, whose eyes held a blend of empathy and shared pain.
"I know the sorrow of losing a home," Fatima said gently.
"Perhaps we can help each other in small ways."

Maria's initial response was cold, driven by bitterness.
"You speak of kindness," she retorted, *"but we have lost everything."*

Fatima's quiet strength did not waver.
"Together, perhaps, we can rebuild hope," she insisted. *"It is fragile, but it is all we have."*

Building Bridges Over Bitterness

The harsh reality of occupation filled Maria's days with humiliation and struggle. In the bustling market one day, a vendor refused to serve her because she was a Christian. Anger and shame burned within her, but Ibrahim, the Ottoman soldier, intervened.
"The war is over," he said firmly. *"This city belongs to all of us now."*

Maria's pain burst forth:
"You speak of peace, but what have you given us except suffering?"

Ibrahim's response was unexpectedly soft, almost pleading:
"I did not wish for this suffering. Perhaps we can choose a different path."

In that moment, Maria glimpsed a truth—perhaps even the conquerors bore the weight of what had been lost.

Years later, Maria found herself at a well being restored for all to use. There, she saw Fatima once more, offering water to both friends and strangers.
"Water belongs to everyone," Fatima said, her voice carrying a simple wisdom. *"Just as hope does."*

Something shifted within Maria, her heart opening in a way she hadn't thought possible.
"Perhaps I judged you too quickly," she admitted. *"We both chose to stay, didn't we?"*
They embraced, not as enemies, but as two women who had chosen reconciliation over bitterness.

Reflections on Loss and Resilience

Reflecting on it all, Maria's gaze is both weary and resolute.
"The fall of Constantinople was not just the collapse of walls; it was the loss of a way of life, a tearing apart of what we believed could never be broken," she confesses.
"But amidst the ruins, there were moments when even the hardest hearts softened, when reconciliation felt possible, however fragile."

Elder Michael's words return to her, filled with the wisdom of time:
"The fall of Constantinople was more than walls crumbling; it was a way of life lost. But amidst

the ruins, new beginnings emerged. Can we find the strength to choose understanding over division?"

With tears in her eyes, Maria's voice carries one final plea:
"This city, my home, taught me that even in the deepest sorrow, there can be a spark of hope. It taught me that true victory lies not in conquest, but in the courage to rebuild and to forgive. May we all find that strength."

And as she stands there, her story resonates as more than a tale of defeat; it is a testament to resilience, faith, and the enduring will to reconcile in the face of irreparable loss.

Conclusion

I am Maria, and the fall of Constantinople was the unraveling of everything we held dear. But even in darkness, moments of humanity emerged: Ibrahim's regret, Fatima's empathy, and shared survival. We learned to coexist not as conquerors and conquered, but as people finding common ground.

The loss will never fully heal, but it taught us lessons: that even amidst ruin, we can rebuild hope together. History's wounds run deep, but the choice to heal remains. Constantinople fell, but its spirit did not. We are the living testament to both loss and resilience. And as long as we hold onto hope, peace is possible—even after conquest."

CHAPTER 14

Playback Theatre

"The Veil of Empire: Echoes of Colonialism in Muslim Lands"

Introduction: Colonization of Muslim Societies (19th Century)

By the 19th century, European colonial powers had penetrated deep into **Muslim lands**, such as **Egypt, Sudan, Libya, Algeria, Indonesia,** and **Central Asia**. Western systems reshaped societies, and the **veil** became a target of **"unveiling campaigns,"** symbolizing resistance against forced cultural assimilation.

The stage is dim, and a single spotlight falls on **Ali**, a local merchant from **Cairo**. He stands tall but carries the weight of the past on his shoulders. His face is etched with sorrow, yet his eyes burn with **defiance and hope**. His voice breaks the silence, carrying the pain of a people under colonial rule.

Ali's voice, choked with anguish, emerges like a cry from a wounded heart:
"I am Ali, a merchant, a son of Cairo, and a witness to the encroaching darkness of the British Empire. They came not just for our land, but for our souls, our identity, our very way of life. The beating heart of Cairo, with all its colors and sounds, fell silent the day they arrived."

Ali's eyes, distant and haunted, carry the pain of memories that refuse to fade. His mind returns to the **bustling markets of Cairo**, where life once brimmed with the rhythms of familiar voices and laughter, now replaced by the heavy march of **foreign boots**. Each step felt like a desecration—an invasion not just of space, but of **spirit**. **Goods were seized, orders barked**, and the pulse of a proud people was subdued. **Fear**, cold and unyielding, choked his voice, leaving his will trapped behind trembling lips.

"I heard Colonel Jameson's voice above the oppressive silence. His words, hollow yet commanding, reached through the chaos: 'We are here to bring order, but this is their home, not just our conquest.' But even he, beneath his rigid exterior, seemed to recognize the theft—of land, of stories, of an ancient way of life. It was not order; it was a forced amnesia."

Ali's voice, though soft, carries the weight of **loss and anger** as he recalls the transformation of Cairo's streets. **Once adorned with flowing Arabic script, they now bore foreign letters and names.** The intrusion felt like a **silent erasure of centuries of heritage**, like watching one's soul being rewritten in an alien tongue.

"Amina," he remembers with a surge of admiration, **"stood defiant, refusing to remove her veil—a symbol of her dignity. 'You may rule my land,' she told the officers, 'but you cannot conquer my spirit.'** Her courage was a whisper of resistance, a reminder that while they could control our land, they could not claim our souls."

Ali himself, unable to contain the simmering rage, stood before the colonial officials one day. His words were **raw, burning with the truth of centuries**: **"This is not progress; this is theft."**

But he was met with the same **cold disdain**, as if he were merely an obstacle—a relic from a past they sought to bury beneath foreign flags.

Yet amid the darkness, hope flickered.

In **secret corners**, poets and storytellers gathered to keep Cairo's spirit alive. **Fatima**, a woman of unwavering resolve, would whisper:
"They can take our lands, but not our stories."

Her words were more than defiance; they were a **declaration of survival**. A poet's haunting chant echoed in these clandestine gatherings:
"'They came with guns and gold, but within our hearts, the fire still burns.'"
It was a promise, a silent vow that the heritage of Cairo would endure, unyielding.

The Uprising

And then came the uprising. The streets of Cairo, like a dormant volcano, erupted with the **fury of a people reclaiming their voice.**
Amina's cry pierced the air:
"This land is ours! We fight for our children and our faith."

Her bravery was contagious, the **fire in her eyes igniting a wave of courage among the crowd.**
Ali, injured but resolute, continued to chant:

"Freedom is worth the pain, for those who come after."

Even **Colonel Jameson**, in the midst of the chaos, seemed torn—his eyes revealing a humanity that contradicted the empire's cruel ambitions.

The Aftermath

In the aftermath, Cairo was **scarred but unbroken**.
"We claimed to bring light," Ali recalls Colonel Jameson saying with a voice heavy with regret, **"but all I see is darkness."**

It was the **admission of a man who had seen both conquest and consequence.** The empire's legacy, written in the ruins of the city, could not erase the spirit that remained.

Ali's gaze turns inward, his voice filled with **pride and sorrow:**
"They took our land, but not our courage. We are a people of stories, of heritage, of unbreakable spirit."
Fatima's words echo within him: "Our stories, our faith will live on, stronger than any empire."

Conclusion

"The Veil of Empire is not only about the domination of land but an **assault on identity, culture, and spirit.** Empires rise and fall, but true resistance is born from **love of culture, faith, and people.** Even amid forced assimilation, the oppressed clung to their **traditions and stories.** While colonial powers left scars, they could not conquer the **human heart.**

This story reminds us that **empires fade, but the spirit of the people endures, carrying forward hope for freedom, dignity, and cultural restoration."**

CHAPTER 15

Playback Theatre – "Exile of the Homeland: The Palestinian Displacement"

"Exile of the Homeland: The Palestinian Displacement"

Introduction

In 1947, the **United Nations** proposed a partition plan to create separate **Jewish and Arab states in Palestine**. Jewish leaders accepted the plan, but **Arab leaders rejected it**, foreseeing the potential displacement of their people. This decision led to conflict, culminating in the declaration of the **state of Israel on May 14, 1948.** The declaration triggered military intervention by neighboring Arab states, sparking the 1948 **Arab-Israeli War**—referred to by Palestinians as the **Nakba**, or "catastrophe." This conflict resulted in the **forced displacement of over 700,000 Palestinian Arabs**, transforming the landscape and identity of the region.

The stage is dimly lit, with **Noura**, a Palestinian mother, standing alone. Her face is etched with the **pain of loss and exile**, but her eyes carry a faint, flickering hope. She takes a deep breath, preparing to recount a tale of profound **heartache and resilience**.

Noura's Story

Noura's voice, filled with a deep, resonating sorrow, begins like a whisper of lost dreams:
"I am Noura, a mother, a survivor, a witness to the exile of my people in 1947-48. It was more than the loss of land; it was the uprooting of our very being, the tearing away of our identity. Everything we knew as home was taken from us, leaving us as wanderers in a foreign landscape. Yet, amid the pain, a small flame of hope refused to die—a hope that one day, somehow, we would return."

Noura's words tremble as she remembers the day the United Nations voted to partition Palestine. Her mind drifts back to that moment when her whole village gathered around a crackling radio. The air was filled with **anxiety**, and the room with her family's silent prayers.

The announcement felt like a dagger, sharp and final:
"They are dividing our land... the land of our ancestors, the soil that held our stories and buried our loved ones. How can they decide this? How can they take away what has been ours for centuries?"

Noura's heart shattered, but her son, **Hassan**, refused to surrender to despair.
"This is our home!" he had shouted, his young voice defiant against the encroaching darkness.
"No decree, no boundary can make us leave. This is the land where I was born, and it is where I will die."

His words were filled with youthful courage, but in Noura's heart, she sensed a storm approaching—a storm that would change their lives forever.

The Exodus

The exodus came suddenly, shrouded in the terror of **gunfire**, the distant **roar of tanks**, and the **panicked cries of neighbors.**
Noura recalls the night as if it were happening again: the **urgent need to flee**, to protect her children from a fate unknown.
"Quickly, my darlings," she had urged, her voice cracking under the weight of fear. **"Take only what you can carry. We must leave now, or there may be no tomorrow."**

Her daughter, **Amal**, clutched a small doll to her chest, her innocent eyes wide with confusion.
"Mama, why do we have to leave? Will we ever come back?"

The question, filled with the simple longing of a child, broke Noura's heart.
Hassan, standing at the door with fierce determination, made a promise:
"We will return, Amal. This is our land, and we will come back."

But as they joined the **long line of refugees**, Noura knew they were stepping into an **uncertain void**, carrying the unbearable weight of displacement.

Life in Exile

Life in exile was a stark existence, reduced to **mere survival within the confines of a bleak refugee camp in Lebanon.**

Noura's voice grows weary as she recalls those early days—**days of endless waiting, makeshift shelters, and the silent mourning of a life left behind.**

"We are still together, Amal," she tried to reassure her daughter. **"As long as we are together, we are home."**

But Amal's reply, simple yet piercing, revealed the depth of her grief: **"Mama, this is not home. It's just a tent. I miss our village, my friends, and our garden."**

Noura's heart ached with a longing she could not ease, a longing that could not be replaced by mere words.
Hassan, on the other hand, **seethed with frustration**, his spirit too wild for the confinement of exile.
"We cannot accept this as our fate," he insisted. **"We must fight for our right to return. We will not let the world forget us."**
His defiance was a fragile beacon, illuminating the darkness with a determination to be seen, to exist.

Memories and Resistance

In the face of despair, Noura found strength in **memories**—memories that were not just fragments of a lost past, but **roots that ran deep, impossible to sever.**
"Our land is like our heart," she often recited, her voice carrying the wisdom of old Palestinian verses.
"Even if they burn our trees, the roots remain, and one day they will bloom again."

Amal, inspired by her mother's words, began to draw pictures of their village on scraps of paper.
"When we return, I will plant new trees in our garden," she said softly, her voice filled with a fragile hope.

Meanwhile, Hassan channeled his anger into action, joining young men in acts of resistance.
"We may be in exile," he declared, **"but we are not defeated. The world must hear us; this injustice cannot last forever."**

Struggle for Recognition

Noura's voice rises with fiery determination as she recalls the relentless struggle for recognition.

Years passed, but the longing for their homeland never faded. In the streets of Jerusalem, during protests and marches, their voices rose above years of silence and hardship.
"We have not given up, and we never will," Noura proclaimed at one demonstration, her words echoing with the fervor of generations.

Amal, now a young woman, stood beside her, holding a sign that read:
"We are not just refugees; we are Palestinians, and we will return."

It was not just a protest; it was an **affirmation of identity**, an assertion of belonging that no decree could erase.

Conclusion

As Noura reaches the final moments of her story, her voice softens, filled with both pride and vulnerability.
"We may have lost our homes, but not our spirit," she reflects, her eyes shining with tears that speak of both pain and resilience.
"We have survived exile, and that means we are stronger than ever."

Speaking to the younger generation in the camp, she urges them to hold onto hope, to never forget where they came from.
Amal, inspired by her mother's resilience, makes a solemn vow:
"We may be scattered, but our hearts are united. One day, we will break the chains of exile and find our way home."

Epilogue: "The Memory of the Land"

"The displacement of Palestinians was not just a geographical shift but a human tragedy. Over 7 million of us were uprooted, scattered across borders. But through all the pain, the longing for return remains strong—a testament to the enduring spirit of a people who refuse to forget, who hold onto hope despite the weight of history. Can we, as witnesses to this story, find the courage to foster dialogue, understanding, and healing?"

CHAPTER 16

Healing Phobias with the Atonement of Yeshua

The Return of John Romeo

John Romeo reappeared on the screen, his face resolute beneath the **Great Banner of Healing**. The words behind him radiated a sense of urgency: "**Healing the Descendants of Abraham.**" He stood tall, his voice filled with earnest conviction as he addressed the assembly.

"**My brothers and sisters,**" he began, "today, we gather not just as descendants of Abraham, but as people carrying the weight of centuries of conflicts. These conflicts have taken the form of wars, violence, and bloodshed—missiles being fired, bombs dropped, and innocent lives lost. We have seen Abrahamic brothers and sisters warring against one another, spilling each other's blood."

He paused, letting the weight of his words sink in. "**These acts of destruction have not only caused physical damage but have left deep spiritual scars, casting shadows over lands and hearts that once sought divine light.**"

The Modern Struggle: A Landscape of Phobias

John's tone became somber as he continued. "**In recent times, we have seen the emergence of phobias that have further divided us—deep-rooted hatreds and misunderstandings that only serve to worsen the pain.**"

1. **Christophobia**: "It represents a visceral dislike for Christians, their beliefs, and their rituals," he explained. "A fear born out of past crusades, colonial impositions, and misunderstandings. It has created divisions where there should have been unity."
2. **Islamophobia**: "This phobia, rooted in suspicion, casts Muslims as 'others,' driven by a lack of understanding of their traditions and the perception of violence tied to events such as 9/11. **It distorts the reality that Islam, at its core, preaches peace and compassion.**"
3. **Hinduphobia**: "This stems from a misunderstanding of Hinduism's diverse rituals and polytheistic traditions. There are those who cannot comprehend the myriad

deities or the philosophies of the Vedas, leading to prejudice."

4. **Jew Phobia or Anti-Semitism**: "And then, there is the oldest and most persistent hatred: anti-Semitism—a deep-seated hostility toward Jews. **This phobia has existed for millennia, from the time of the Egyptians, Assyrians, and Babylonians, to the Holocaust of the 20th century.**"

John paused, his eyes reflecting the pain of these divisions. "**But perhaps the most pivotal moment that intensified anti-Semitism was the crucifixion of Yeshua. This great act of selfless love demonstrated by Yeshua became a central narrative that polarized Jewish and Christian communities for centuries.**"

The Crucifixion of Yeshua: A Turning Point

The screen dimmed, and a powerful image of Yeshua on the cross appeared, accompanied by a haunting, yet beautiful melody. John's voice softened, filled with reverence as he narrated, "**It was the Jewish high priests, the Pharisees, and the Sanhedrin who brought Yeshua to the Roman authorities, accusing him of blasphemy. To them, he was a threat—a man who spoke of love for enemies, of inclusion, and of a kingdom not of this world.**"

The audience was immersed in the scene, feeling the rawness of Yeshua's sacrifice. "**He was brought before Pontius Pilate, the Roman governor, and despite Pilate's own doubts about the accusations, Yeshua was sentenced to death by crucifixion. It was a gruesome and humiliating death meant for criminals and rebels.**"

Yeshua's Message of Unconditional Love

John's voice grew more intense. "**The crucifixion of Yeshua is often cited as one of humanity's greatest sins. And yet, within this great sin, God's grace abounded. Yeshua, the Lion of Judah, did not die in defeat; he died in triumph, offering a path of unconditional love that transcended human sinfulness.**"

The image on the screen shifted to a radiant vision of Yeshua resurrected, standing in a golden light. "**In his death, Yeshua demonstrated a love so powerful, so all-encompassing, that it became a beacon for the world. He taught us to love our enemies, to embrace those who hate us, and to sacrifice** ourselves for others."

John looked directly into the camera, his eyes filled with passion. **"This is the essence of unconditional love—a love that heals, restores, and binds even the most broken of relationships."**

Playback Theatre: Yeshua's Story Reenacted

To bring this message home, John introduced a **Playback Theatre segment** titled **"The Agony and Love of Yeshua."** The scene was set in Jerusalem, with Yeshua speaking to his disciples. The actors portrayed the pain, betrayal, and ultimate sacrifice with raw emotion.

Yeshua's Testimony - The Price of Unconditional Love

The digital screen glowed softly as a figure appeared, dressed simply, with a face that seemed to carry both infinite tenderness and the weight of untold burdens. It was **Yeshua himself**, stepping into the virtual world to tell his own story. He stood with a quiet strength, his eyes filled with both compassion and authority.

"My name is Yeshua," he began, **his voice resonating through the vast digital coliseum. "My father is Joseph, and my mother is Mary,"** he continued, **with a humility that belied the gravity of his mission.**

He paused, letting his words sink in, as if inviting the audience to journey back in time with him. **"My father is the 42nd generation from Abraham. Between me and the Babylonian Exile, there were 14 generations; another 14 generations between the Babylonian Exile and King David; and 14 more from King David to the patriarch Abraham."**

Yeshua's voice grew more solemn, his tone imbued with a sense of divine destiny. **"My birth was foretold 400 years before it happened. The prophet Isaiah proclaimed that a child would be born, a mighty king and counselor, upon whose shoulders the government would rest."** His gaze seemed to reach through the screens, touching the souls of all who were watching. **"This prophecy was fulfilled in Bethlehem, where I was born, and in Nazareth, where I grew up."**

The Preparation: Nazareth, Qumran, and the Essenes

Yeshua continued with a sense of nostalgia, yet with an undercurrent of destiny. **"In my early years, I was shaped by the traditions of Nazareth, yet I also spent time in the wilderness with the Essenes at Qumran, near the Dead Sea. It was a period of preparation, a time of spiritual growth and contemplation."**

He painted a vivid picture of his years spent studying and meditating, growing not only in wisdom but in spiritual depth. **"The Essenes were seekers of truth, and their devotion inspired me. I learned from them the importance of purity, simplicity, and a deep, abiding connection to God."**

Yeshua's voice took on a tone of anticipation as he reached a pivotal moment in his life. **"When I was 30 years old, I went down to the Jordan River, where my cousin John was baptizing. I stepped into the waters, and as I was baptized, the heavens opened. God's Spirit descended upon me like a dove, and a voice declared, 'This is my beloved Son, in whom I am well pleased.'"**

The First Miracles: Water into Wine and Beyond

The screen behind Yeshua flickered with images of Cana. **"Soon after my baptism, I was at a wedding feast in Cana,"** he continued. **"When the wine ran out, I transformed water into wine, allowing the celebration to continue. This was my first public miracle, a sign of God's abundance and joy."**

Yeshua's face softened as he recounted this moment of divine grace. **"But that was only the beginning,"** he said. **"I then healed the royal official's son in Galilee—he was healed from a distance, with just a word spoken from my lips. In the synagogue at Capernaum, I cast out an unclean spirit from a possessed man, and the people marveled at the authority I possessed. Word spread quickly, and the people began to follow me."**

The Rejection at Nazareth: A Heartfelt Sorrow

Yeshua's expression grew more somber as he recounted a painful memory. **"I returned to Nazareth, my hometown, and went to the synagogue on the Sabbath. They handed me the scroll of Isaiah, and I read: 'The Spirit of the Lord is upon me, because He has anointed me to preach the gospel to the poor, to heal the brokenhearted, to proclaim liberty to the captives, and recovery of sight to the blind, to set at liberty those who are oppressed, to** proclaim the acceptable year of the Lord.'"

Yeshua paused, his eyes filled with a quiet anguish. **"When I finished reading, I declared to them that the scripture was fulfilled in their hearing. But instead of rejoicing, they were offended. They could not accept that someone from their own town could be the anointed one. They drove me out of the synagogue, attempting to throw me off a cliff."**

The pain in his voice was palpable. **"But the Spirit of God was with me, and I walked right through the crowd, untouched. Yes, my people rejected me—those I had come to save were the very ones who turned against me."**

Confronting the Pharisees and Sadducees: A Clash of Truths

Yeshua's tone grew firmer as he spoke of the religious leaders of his time. **"The Pharisees, with their legalism and rituals, believed they were righteous, but their hearts were far from God. They were proud of their public prayers and their adherence to the law, yet they looked down on the common people, seeing them as unworthy."**

His eyes narrowed slightly, filled with righteous indignation. **"And then there were the Sadducees—the aristocrats, closely aligned with the Roman authorities. They denied the resurrection, the existence of angels, and even the Spirit of God. They controlled the temple and used it for political gain."**

Yeshua's voice took on a tone of confrontation. **"I called them 'vipers' and 'whitewashed tombs' because they led the people deeper into spiritual darkness, using rituals to bind rather than liberate. When I healed on the Sabbath, they were enraged. They accused me of breaking the law, even though the Sabbath was meant for rest, healing, and renewal."**

The Triumphal Entry: Cheered by the Crowds, Feared by the Authorities

The screen showed scenes of Yeshua's entry into Jerusalem, riding on a donkey as people laid palm branches before him, shouting, **"Hosanna!"** Yeshua's voice took on a note of sadness mixed with hope. **"The people welcomed me as a king, but the Pharisees and Sadducees were threatened. They conspired against me, plotting my death."**

He described the betrayal by Judas, one of his closest followers. **"While I prayed in Gethsemane, Judas approached with soldiers and kissed me, marking me for arrest. I was taken to Caiaphas, the high priest, and then to Pontius Pilate."**

The Brutal Path to Calvary: The Agony of Yeshua's Sacrifice

Yeshua's voice became deep with sorrow as he began recounting the final and most excruciating part of his journey.

"After three years of my mission, I entered Jerusalem, riding on a humble donkey. The people, filled with hope, cheered my arrival, laying palm branches in my path and shouting, 'Hosanna!' Yet, not everyone was pleased. The Pharisees and Sadducees were threatened by my presence, by the love and truth I represented."

The screen behind him depicted the jubilant crowd, contrasting sharply with the tense expressions of the religious leaders who looked on with suspicion. Yeshua continued, his tone filled with a mixture of determination and sadness.

"The leaders, led by the Sanhedrin, conspired against me. On that fateful night, while I prayed in the Garden of Gethsemane, Judas, one of my own apostles, betrayed me with a kiss—identifying me to the authorities."

The audience was riveted, sensing the pain in every word Yeshua spoke.

"Roman guards, guided by the Sanhedrin, arrested me and brought me before Caiaphas, the high priest. From there, I was taken to Annas, then back to Caiaphas, and finally handed over to Pontius Pilate. I was paraded from one authority to another, accused of blasphemy by the Jewish leaders who sought my death."

The Torture at the Hands of Pilate

Yeshua's voice became graver as he described his trial before Pilate.

"Pilate, unsure of my guilt, ordered me to be beaten. They pulled the beard from my face, as it was foretold by Isaiah, until my cheeks were exposed to the bone. It was painful, and the humiliation was deep. They mocked me, placing a brutish crown of thorns upon my head. They pressed it down with such force that the thorns pierced my scalp and eyes, blinding me with blood and excruciating pain."

The screen showed the brutal imagery, and the audience could almost feel the horror of the moment. Yeshua continued; his tone unwavering despite the torment he described.

"They ripped my back with lashes embedded with shards of bone. Each lash plowed through my skin until it was a bleeding mess. My body was broken, my strength almost gone."

Yeshua paused, allowing the gravity of his suffering to sink in.

"Pilate, still uncertain of what to do with me, sent me to Herod, who had jurisdiction over the region. But Herod, swayed by the demands of the Jewish leaders, decreed my crucifixion. He fulfilled their wish, labeling me a heretic and a blasphemer, condemning me under Jewish law."

The Journey to Calvary

Yeshua's face tightened with the memory of the journey to Calvary.

"From Herod's court, they handed me a heavy wooden cross, forcing me to carry it through the streets of Jerusalem. My body was half-dead, my wounds still bleeding, and my spirit heavy. With each step, I struggled to keep moving forward, burdened by the weight of the cross and the pain that racked my body."

The screen now displayed images of the crowded streets, with spectators jeering and mocking. Yeshua's voice grew softer but remained steady.

"As I stumbled under the load, Simon of Cyrene was compelled by the guards to help me carry the cross. His unexpected act of kindness allowed me to regain some strength, even as my body faltered."

Yeshua's voice broke slightly as he recalled the faces of two men who stood in the distance.

"From afar, I saw Joseph of Arimathea and Nicodemus—both Pharisees who had come to understand my mission. Tears streamed down their faces as they watched me suffer, unable to intervene."

The Crucifixion: The Agony on the Cross

The tone of Yeshua's voice became faint, filled with exhaustion, as he relived the final moments of his life.

"When we reached Calvary, they laid the cross on the ground and stretched my arms over the beams. They tied my wrists, then drove a thick nail through

each wrist, pinning me to the cross.”

The audience gasped, the weight of the moment pressing down on them.
“With me still nailed to the beams, they raised the cross upright, making me hang from the top. My body convulsed with pain as the weight pulled against the nails in my wrists. Breathing became nearly impossible, each breath an agonizing effort.”

Yeshua’s voice grew hoarse, mirroring the pain he had endured.
“Finally, they drove another nail through my feet, nailing me to the cross completely. I hung there, gasping for air, crying out in agony.”

The silence in the digital coliseum was absolute, as the audience struggled to grasp the depth of the sacrifice being described. Yeshua’s next words came slowly, each one a testament to his suffering.
“The pain was unbearable, my heart struggling to beat under the strain. I knew that my mission was reaching its end, and with one final cry, I said, ‘It is finished.’ My heart burst, unable to withstand the torment any longer.”

The Silence of the Cross: An Unfathomable Sacrifice

Yeshua’s last words lingered in the air, and the audience was overcome with emotion. There was no sound, no movement—only a deep, soul-stirring silence. It was as if the weight of the cross had been placed upon the hearts of every listener, each one feeling the agony and love that had driven Yeshua to such a sacrifice.

It was not just a retelling; it was a moment of living history—a confrontation with the raw, unfiltered reality of what Yeshua had endured to redeem humanity.

The audience watched in silence, some with tears streaming down their faces, as the profound message of Yeshua’s love filled the virtual space.

From Phobias to Healing

John’s voice returned, filled with renewed energy.
“Healing the descendants of Abraham means we must move beyond phobias and hatreds. We must allow the unconditional love of Yeshua to enter our hearts, for only love can break the cycle of fear.”

He then led the audience through a moment of collective prayer, calling for the spirit of Abraham to fill each participant with love, peace, and understanding.

"May the spirit of Yeshua guide us," he prayed, "to embrace our enemies, to overcome our biases, and to heal the wounds of our past. Let us be instruments of peace, carrying the light of Abraham's promise to the darkest corners of the world."

Manjula Devaraj's Call to Action

As John stepped back, Manjula Devaraj reappeared, her eyes glowing with determination.
"We have witnessed the story of Yeshua's ultimate act of love," she began. "But now, we must turn this story into action."

She called for the creation of interfaith dialogues, not just as mere discussions, but as platforms for reconciliation.
"We need to build centers of healing, where descendants of Abraham can come together, share their stories, and find common ground."

"Let us organize peace marches, where Muslims, Jews, Christians, Hindus, and people of all faiths can walk side by side, demonstrating our shared commitment to peace. Let us host interfaith prayer vigils, offering prayers for one another's well-being."

The Abrahamic Family Pledge

Manjula led the participants once more in the **Abrahamic Family Pledge**:
"I pledge to embrace love, reject fear, and work tirelessly to heal the wounds of the past."

As the pledge was repeated by thousands of participants around the world, a sense of hope and renewal filled the virtual conclave. The words became more than a promise; they became a commitment to live the essence of Yeshua's teachings.

A New Dawn for the Descendants of Abraham

The session closed with the uplifting **Abrahamic Theme Song**, filling the digital airwaves with a sense of joy and unity. Participants from different nations, races, and religions sang along, their voices blending into a universal harmony.

John Romeo's final words lingered, touching every soul present:
"Let us be the generation that heals the wounds of the past, for the descendants of Abraham are not just called to be survivors, but to be the

bringers of peace and the bearers of love in a broken world."
"To Shine like Stars, Guiding the World."

John Romeo's Call to the World: Understanding the Sacrifice

John Romeo stepped back into view, his hands raised to calm the audience. His face was marked by awe and deep emotion.
"Friends," he began, his voice filled with reverence, "we must not only understand the sacrifice of Yeshua but embrace it. It was not merely a tragic event, but the greatest act of love—a love that brought us from darkness into Yeshua's kingdom of light."

His tone grew somber as he addressed the lingering effects of Yeshua's death.
"This act of redemption, however, became the root of anti-Semitism. For centuries, the Jews were blamed for the crucifixion, leading to unspeakable hatred and persecution, including the Holocaust. The stigma persisted, even through the Reformation led by Martin Luther, who harbored deep resentment against the Jewish people."

A Plea to Eradicate Anti-Semitism: Healing Old Wounds

John Romeo's voice carried a deep plea.
"This bias, this prejudice against the Jewish people, must be eradicated. It is rooted in the misunderstanding of Yeshua's sacrifice. Abraham was spared from sacrificing his son, but God, in His love for humanity, did not spare His own. He gave Yeshua to the world to break the chains of sin and establish unconditional love."

The screen displayed scenes of modern conflicts, and Romeo's voice echoed with urgency.
"The state of Israel, though often criticized and politically controversial, is still a recipient of Yeshua's love. Whether they accept Yeshua as the Messiah or not, the love of Yeshua is for everyone—believer or not."

He paused, looking directly into the camera.
"The world must understand this truth: Yeshua's sacrifice was not about blame but about redemption. If we can grasp this, we can begin to heal the wounds of anti-Semitism that have persisted for centuries."

The Global Silence: A Moment of Reflection

The participants, representing diverse backgrounds and faiths, were stunned into a profound silence. Yeshua's words, coupled with John Romeo's call for reconciliation, created a moment of deep reflection. It was as if the digital world itself had paused, as hearts across the globe grappled with the weight of the message.

The Resurrection of Hope: A Mighty Roar of Praise

Suddenly, a powerful roar erupted from the audience. It was a spontaneous outpouring of emotion, a cry that rose from the depths of human hearts everywhere.
"Yeshua, King of Kings and Lord of Lords!" they shouted, voices mingling with tears of joy and relief.

As if in response, the heavens seemed to open. Angelic voices were imagined to join the earthly chorus, singing praises to the One who had paid the ultimate price for humanity's redemption. It was a moment that transcended time and space, a merging of earthly and divine praise.

A Call to Action: Embracing Unconditional Love

John Romeo stood tall, his face beaming with hope.
"Brothers and sisters," he declared, his voice filled with conviction, **"Yeshua's sacrifice was not just a past event. It is a living reality that continues to offer redemption and love. We are called to embody this love, to break down barriers, and to bring healing to a world that still suffers from hatred and division."**

The chapter ended not with a quiet conclusion, but with a roaring call to action. Hearts were awakened, eyes filled with tears, and voices raised in praise. It was a global awakening, a realization that the love of Yeshua was not just for the past but for the present—a force capable of transforming individuals, nations, and the very fabric of humanity.

It was not just the end of a chapter; it was the beginning of a **revolution of love,** a call to embody the legacy of Yeshua, to heal the wounds of history, and to establish a world where **unconditional love reigns supreme.**

SECTION D– EMPOWERING THE DESCENDANTS OF ABRAHAM

CHAPTER 17

Day Three of the Global Virtual Conclave (Morning Session)

The **third and final day** of the global virtual conclave of the Yeshuans was about to begin. The air was charged with anticipation, as thousands gathered virtually from every corner of the world, representing the **descendants of Abraham**. The global audience, appearing as countless faces on the big screens, eagerly awaited the unfolding of what promised to be a historic and transformative moment.

The massive screen lit up, and **Yaseva, the Convener of the Yeshuan Movement**, appeared, radiating a sense of calm authority. His presence commanded the space, and the gathering fell silent. With a broad smile and an open heart, he greeted the assembly:

"Descendants of Abraham worldwide! My dear friends, brothers, and sisters, we stand together today, as numerous as the stars in the sky, just as it was promised. We have arrived at this third and final day of our conclave, a gathering unlike any that has come before—a landmark event in our shared history. And while this conclave may be one of a kind, Yeshua's assurance is that even greater things lie ahead, for he told us, 'You will do greater things than these.' This is his promise, his assurance for us all."

As the audience sat in rapt attention, **Yaseva recapped the remarkable journey** of the conclave so far:

"From the moment we began, we traced the exponential expansion of the descendants of Abraham. What started as a small, three-fold covenant has now unfolded to encompass the entire planet. It is clear that everyone who carries love within their hearts is a rightful claimant of Abraham's blessing—an eternal nation without boundaries, defined not by geography but by a shared commitment to love, compassion, and justice. This is our calling, and it is a glorious calling!"

The Transformative First Day

Yaseva's voice grew softer, yet more resonant, as he relived the power of the first day:

"The first day was marked by immense beauty, as we recognized the scale of this expansion. We witnessed how the promise of Abraham has reached not only Jews, Christians, and Muslims but also millions beyond these faiths—people who embody love and thus belong to this eternal nation of God's children. We reflected on how love has truly become the unifying force, transcending cultural and religious divides."

The crowd felt a renewed surge of inspiration, recalling the sense of unity and promise that filled the virtual halls on that opening day.

The Healing Power of the Second Day

Yaseva then shifted to the events of the second day, his tone taking on a deeper, more solemn reverence:

"Yesterday, we entered the realm of healing. Through the extraordinary medium of playback theater, we revisited the most traumatic chapters of our collective history, spanning generations and millennia. We courageously confronted the pain, the betrayals, and the countless struggles that have shaped our story. And above all, we heard Yeshua himself, recounting the monumental story of his sacrifice—explaining the 'why,' the 'how,' and the immense purpose behind his offering."

His words pierced the hearts of the listeners, evoking memories of the vivid reenactments that had brought tears to many. The spiritual catharsis was tangible, echoing across screens, with each participant feeling the weight and subsequent release of centuries of division and suffering.

"Yeshua's sacrifice established unconditional love as the ultimate power on this Earth, binding us together as one people. His love was not limited to his followers but extended even to those who condemned him. And yesterday, this truth came alive among us, cleansing the deep-rooted spirit of anti-Semitism that has plagued humanity. We acknowledged our debt to the Jewish people, who gifted us with Yeshua, the Son of God, the King of Kings, the Prince of Peace. Today, we thank God for healing humanity of this grave oppression, removing the stain of division and elevating the Jews as the proud ancestors of this great gift to the world."

There was a palpable sense of gratitude, awe, and reverence, as **Yaseva's words resonated** through the virtual assembly, bridging centuries of pain with newfound reconciliation.

The Mission of the Third Day

Now, Yaseva's voice grew firm and resolute, as he prepared to outline the purpose of this final day:
"Today, we stand at a momentous juncture. We are called not merely to reflect, but to act. Yeshua taught us that faith without action is dead, and so we must be the living embodiment of his message. Our work is needed in a world where God's love, grace, and mercy must be extended to all. We have been given a clear mission—to build a world of joy, justice, and unity. But to achieve this, we must commit to action with the same fervor that has brought us here."

He paused, letting the weight of his words sink in.

"It is with this spirit that we now welcome a fellow Yeshuan, Commander Abdul Rauf, a former commander of the Indian Navy. He has since devoted his life to our cause and carries a bold vision of spreading peace, joy, and unity across nations. His mission is to establish what he calls a 'Joy Dome'—a spiritual shield that will encompass the descendants of Abraham, offering protection, hope, and strength."

The virtual crowd burst into applause as **Yaseva introduced Abdul Rauf**, a man who had seen both the harsh realities of military service and the transcendent power of spiritual awakening.

Commander Abdul Rauf's Call to Action

Abdul Rauf took the stage, a charismatic presence exuding both strength and humility. He began by sharing his personal transformation from a life of military discipline to a life driven by faith and compassion.

"My friends, in my years of service, I saw conflict, pain, and destruction. But it was in the midst of this darkness that I found the light of Yeshua's teachings. His message of love, forgiveness, and reconciliation became my guiding force. Today, I stand before you as not just a former commander, but as a man committed to the mission of peace—a peace that is proactive, expansive, and all-encompassing."

Abdul Rauf then laid out his vision for the **Joy Dome**, a symbolic initiative aimed at bringing tangible relief to regions plagued by strife and division:
"This dome will be more than just an idea; it will be a movement of hope. It will involve building communities of joy through humanitarian aid, spiritual guidance, and grassroots action. We will work tirelessly to ensure that every person, regardless of their background, can experience the love that Yeshua taught us. This is the call of our time, and it is a call that I believe each of you can help answer."

The audience erupted into enthusiastic cheers, acknowledging the boldness of this mission and the clarity of purpose that had emerged over these three days.

The Grand Vision of the 'Joy Dome' Unveiled by Commander Abdul Rauf

Commander Abdul Rauf appeared under a grand banner that read **"Joy Dome: The New Dawn for Humanity."** His aura was that of a warrior turned peacemaker—one whose mission had evolved from defense to universal upliftment. The descendants of Abraham were ready—no longer divided by history's shadows, but united by faith's light, ready to conquer the world not with swords, but with the unbreakable power of love.

"Greetings, my brothers and sisters," he began, his voice filled with passion and urgency. **"Today, I stand before you not just as a commander, but as a messenger of a revolutionary vision. A vision that will reshape not only our communities but the very fabric of global consciousness. I introduce to you the Joy Dome—a concept born out of necessity, fueled by the spirit of hope and unconditional love, and destined to bring about the greatest transformation humanity has ever seen."**

From Defense to Healing: The Birth of the Joy Dome

Commander Rauf paused, taking a deep breath before continuing.
"In a world dominated by conflicts and crises, nations have invested in technologies that primarily protect and defend. The most prominent of these is the Iron Dome, a marvel of military engineering that intercepts incoming missiles to safeguard the people beneath its shield. While this technology has undoubtedly saved lives, it is ultimately a symbol of war, a mechanism that reflects our fear-driven instincts."

His eyes blazed with determination as he moved forward.

"But what if there was something different? Something not designed to intercept missiles but to spread joy? What if there was a shield that didn't just protect, but actively nurtured and uplifted those beneath it? What if, instead of a dome of iron, we could create a Dome of Joy?"

The audience, both virtual and physical, was transfixed, hanging on his every word.

"The Joy Dome is not just a dome; it is a paradigm shift," Rauf declared. **"It is a revolutionary operating system for humanity, one that infuses positive energy into individuals, families, communities, and nations. It envelops people in love, peace, and joy—not as mere concepts, but as living, breathing realities."**

He allowed his words to resonate before continuing, **"Imagine a dome that radiates positivity, creating a shield of joy that fills every aspect of life. This dome does not simply guard against external threats; it restructures the very way we think, feel, and interact with one another. It's not a defense mechanism but a transformation mechanism—an instrument of global healing and enlightenment."**

Unpacking the Joy Dome: A Multidimensional Transformation

Commander Rauf then launched into a comprehensive explanation of how the Joy Dome would work, breaking it down into four core modalities that would revolutionize human life.

1. Education Re-imagined: The Core of Joyful Learning

"First and foremost," Rauf said, **"the Joy Dome redefines education itself.** In today's world, education focuses heavily on knowledge accumulation—facts, figures, and data. While these are important, they are incomplete. What we have neglected is the operating system of the human being—the intrinsic software that drives how we perceive and respond to the world. This software is meant to be powered by joy, but it has been corrupted by fear, anger, and negativity."

His voice deepened with emphasis. **"Under the Joy Dome, education becomes a process of awakening, not just of the mind, but of the heart and soul.** It teaches people how to tap into positivity as a source of personal power. It encourages children to develop empathy and compassion alongside mathematics and science. It trains adults to manage conflicts with a spirit of reconciliation rather than retaliation."

The screen shifted to display visuals of happy children engaged in joyful learning, their faces radiating warmth. **"When joy becomes a central component of education, it nurtures kindness, creativity, and critical thinking.** It creates leaders who are not just knowledgeable, but wise, who understand that true power lies not in conquest but in connection."

2. Health and Well-being: Joy as Medicine

Commander Rauf's tone softened as he moved to the next modality. **"The Joy Dome is not just about emotional well-being; it's also about physical health.** You see, when joy becomes the dominant energy within the body, it heals. The human body is designed to thrive on positive energy. When we are filled with joy, our organs function more efficiently, our immune systems are strengthened, and diseases lose their grip."

He paused, allowing the message to sink in. **"Imagine a world where joy is the primary medicine, a world where hospitals are transformed into centers of joyful healing.** People wouldn't just receive treatments; they would receive upliftment. The Joy Dome would create a space where physical ailments are treated alongside emotional wounds, resulting in true, holistic healing."

3. Employment and Empowerment: Joypreneurs as Catalysts of Change

Rauf's voice grew stronger as he delved into the third modality. **"The Joy Dome would inspire a new wave of Joypreneurs—entrepreneurs whose ventures are rooted in joy and aimed at improving lives.** By focusing on solving real problems through compassionate innovation, Joypreneurs convert challenges into opportunities, not just for profit, but for the common good."

He elaborated, **"Imagine businesses that prioritize well-being over wealth, organizations that measure success not just in financial terms, but in terms of the joy they spread.** The Joy Dome would become a thriving ecosystem of such enterprises, creating jobs that fulfill people's hearts and minds, not just their pockets."

He continued, his voice brimming with optimism, **"Under the Joy Dome, employment is no longer a necessity; it becomes a calling.** People work not out of compulsion, but out of joy. They find fulfillment in their roles because they are part of something larger—a collective mission to spread joy and uplift humanity."

4. The Joyist Circles: Building Communities of Positivity

Commander Rauf's eyes shone as he introduced the concept of Joyist Circles. **"These circles are small, self-sustained communities within the Joy Dome, where individuals come together to foster collective joy.** They operate under a sociocratic system—a decision-making process based on consent rather than majority rule. This ensures that everyone's voice is heard, fostering unity rather than division."

He described how these circles would form at the grassroots level. **"Picture neighborhoods transformed into vibrant Joyist Circles, where residents not only know each other but actively support each other.** Vulnerable groups—children, women, the elderly—receive special protection, and community issues are resolved collaboratively."

His voice grew tender as he described the impact, **"In these circles, no one is alone, no one is left behind.** The spirit of joy binds everyone together, creating a safety net that is both spiritual and practical."

A Vision for the Future: Joy Aligned Nations

Commander Rauf's final words echoed with the power of a true leader. **"The Joy Dome is not just an idea; it is a destiny.** It is the manifestation of our highest calling—to transform the world through joy, to heal wounds that have festered for centuries, and to build nations that are aligned with love. This is our mission, our legacy, and our promise."

The screen displayed a final message: **"Joy: The New Dawn of Humanity,"** accompanied by a radiant image of the Joy Dome glowing above the world, symbolizing the dawn of a new era.

The audience erupted into cheers, applause, and tears of joy. They felt a deep, resonating sense of purpose. The Joy Dome was not just a concept; it was a movement—a movement that each one of them would help build, spreading joy like wildfire across the globe.

With this, the session ended, but the journey had just begun. The descendants of Abraham, once divided by history, were now united by a new vision—a vision where love, peace, and joy would truly conquer all.

Descendants of Abraham—The Pioneers of Joy Dome

Commander Abdul Rauf addressed the significance of this mission for the descendants of Abraham. His words carried the weight of centuries of shared history, conflict, and hope.
"We, who once were divided, shall now lead the world toward unity. The descendants of Abraham—Jews, Christians, and Muslims—shall take the lead in establishing the Joy Dome, turning a legacy of conflict into one of global guidance. We shall rise like the stars that illuminate the night sky, guiding humanity toward a harmonious existence."

A Clarion Call to Action: From the Middle East to the World

Commander Rauf concluded, **"The first Joy Dome will be established in the Middle East, the very heart of Abrahamic history.** It is here that the descendants of Abraham have experienced both glory and suffering. It is here that the healing must begin."

His voice reached its crescendo, filled with an unyielding resolve. **"As descendants of Abraham, we are the ones to lead this revolution.** We have fought battles of old; now, we must lead the battle for joy. The Joy Dome will be our legacy, a testament to the spirit of love that Yeshua and other prophets of the Abrahamic tradition exemplified."

Joy Navy—Waves of Positivity

Commander Abdul Rauf's tone shifted, becoming more animated, as he unveiled the next phase of the vision—the **Joy Navy.** His voice, filled with a sense of urgency and purpose, captured the dynamic spirit of this bold initiative.
"To support the Joy Dome, a new force will not only protect but uplift—sailing across the seas to spread positivity, unity, and peace. This is the Joy Navy. Unlike traditional navies that protect with weapons of war, the Joy Navy will protect humanity with waves of joy and compassion. Its mission is not one of conquest, but one of connection. It will foster compassion, sustainability, and global unity across oceans. **With each wave, it will inspire resilience, promote ocean conservation, and offer support to marginalized**

communities worldwide."

Commander Rauf paused, then elaborated on the **Joy Navy's mission statement,** his words ringing with conviction:
"A tidal wave of positivity connecting humanity and the oceans, fostering a culture of compassion and inclusivity. This is the essence of the Joy Navy. Its presence will be felt in the waters, not by the sound of cannons, but by the waves of kindness that ripple outward. **It will be a fleet where each vessel is a beacon of hope, each sailor an ambassador of peace, and each mission a step toward global harmony."**

He described the multifaceted operations of the Joy Navy, painting a vivid picture of its role in shaping a better world:
"The Joy Navy will engage in ocean cleanup efforts, navigating polluted waters and restoring marine ecosystems to their pristine state. It will educate coastal communities on sustainable fishing practices and maritime stewardship, creating a culture of respect for the oceans that sustain us. The Joy Navy will also conduct community development initiatives, from building schools and clinics in remote coastal areas to setting up mobile libraries and cultural exchange centers. Through these efforts, the Joy Navy will not only protect but elevate lives, bringing education, healthcare, and hope to those who have long been overlooked."

With a confident smile, Commander Rauf outlined the global reach of the **Joy Navy,** emphasizing the strategic placement of its regional hubs:
"In Singapore, Miami, Amsterdam, Cape Town, and Dubai, regional hubs will be established, serving as centers for cultural exchange, multilingual initiatives, and programs that promote universal values. These hubs will not only strengthen local connections but will amplify the Joy Navy's impact through regional initiatives. **By enhancing cultural understanding and fostering global collaboration, the Joy Navy will serve as a living example of what humanity can achieve when driven by joy instead of fear."**

He continued with a tone of promise and aspiration:
"The Joy Navy will be a force that heals, not harms; it will be a fleet that bridges divides, not deepens them. It will be a powerful symbol of the new era we are creating, where the tides of the oceans will no longer be messengers of conflict, but carriers of hope, renewal, and global unity. Just imagine: fleets adorned with symbols of peace, their sails catching not just the wind, but the aspirations of

humanity itself."**

The audience was rapt, their imaginations captured by the powerful imagery of ships sailing not for war, but for the well-being of all.

The Joy Flotilla—Harbingers of Harmony

Commander Abdul Rauf's face beamed with pride as he introduced the heart of the Joy Navy—the **Joy Flotilla.** His voice was filled with an almost childlike excitement, as if he could already see the vibrant sails cutting through the Mediterranean waters.

"The Joy Flotilla will not only navigate the seas but will navigate the hearts of nations," he declared, his voice unwavering. **"Its crew—mediators, counselors, humanitarian workers, and Joy Specialists—will foster a new era of global harmony. They will be trained to not only address crises but to preempt them with compassion, understanding, and kindness.** With careful planning, collaboration, and dedication, this initiative can become a beacon of hope, guiding humanity toward an era of peace. It is not just about deploying ships—it is about deploying joy, courage, and compassion."**

He then made a final, heartfelt appeal, his eyes glistening with emotion:
"Picture the Joy Flotilla, its neon-lit yachts exuding vibrancy and joy, sailing across oceans to heal nations. This is not just a mission—it is a movement. **It is a commitment to a future where faith is a bridge, not a weapon; where humanity is united by love, not divided by hate.** It is a promise to create a world where harmony is not an ideal, but a lived reality. Together, let us empower global harmony through partnership, collaboration, and joy. **Let us set sail toward a world where every wave carries hope and every breeze sings the song of peace."**

As he concluded, the audience was spellbound, their hearts filled with inspiration. The vision of a world transformed by joy, carried on the waves of compassion, was not just a distant dream—it felt within reach.

The room erupted into a standing ovation, a wave of shared hope that echoed Commander Abdul Rauf's words:
"This is not just about saving lives—it's about saving our very humanity."

The applause rose like the tides of the oceans he spoke of, filled with the possibility of a world shaped not by power, but by love. Commander Abdul Rauf stood humbly before the crowd, his face radiating both hope and gratitude, as the echoes of a new era filled the hall—a world where the **power of joy would be the ultimate force for peace.**

CHAPTER 18

Day Three of the Global Virtual Conclave (Afternoon Session)

The Dawn of the Joy Force — A Transformative Vision Unleashed
The atmosphere was electric as Yaseva, the convenor of the Yeshuan movement, stood on the grand stage before an assembly of the faithful and the curious, wondering what more was in store for them. His voice, rich with anticipation and reverence, seemed to resonate beyond the physical space, stirring hearts and minds alike.

"Today," he announced, "we are about to embark on a revolutionary journey—a journey that holds the power to reshape our world. This is not merely an idea; it is a calling to awaken and uplift humanity on a scale we have not dared imagine."

The crowd leaned in, breath held in collective anticipation, as Yaseva introduced a figure who, for over thirty years, had been a close companion, a strategist, and a visionary mind: Manohara.

"Manohara," he continued, "is a master strategist, a thinker with unparalleled insight into technology, digital communication, and human potential. He is here to present to us the concept that will complement our Joy Dome Project—a concept that redefines the very nature of what we know as power and defense."

With that, he gestured toward the stage, and the anticipation grew.

Manohara stepped forward, his presence quiet yet imbued with an uncontainable energy that filled the room.

"Thank you, Yaseva," he began with warmth and humility, "and thank you to each and every one of you, my dear brothers and sisters in the lineage of Abraham. We gather here not as strangers, but as family—each of us bound by love, by the legacy of Abraham, and by a common purpose to bring transformation to this world. Today, I present to you the Joy Force—an innovative paradigm designed to revolutionize defense and national strength. Not just as a protective measure, but as a force for global upliftment, for

healing, and for unity."

The Concept of Joy Force: A New Ethos for Peace

Manohara paused, allowing his words to settle into the minds of his audience.

"Today, nations rely on armed forces—air, land, and sea divisions—that operate with an ethos rooted in ancient times. These forces are descendants of centuries-old warrior mentalities that trace back to the Vikings, the Romans, the Huns, and countless other military empires. While the weapons have evolved—from spears and swords to advanced weaponry—the underlying spirit remains the same: one of conquest and harsh dominance."

He scanned the audience, his gaze penetrating.

"Why do we continue to confine our incredible human resources—soldiers, pilots, sailors, engineers—to roles defined by aggression and violence? Why do we only mobilize these heroes during times of catastrophe or conflict? Imagine a world where these same forces, trained in resilience, skill, and bravery, were given a new mission: to spread joy, to bring peace, and to nurture progress, rather than simply being instruments of war."

The energy in the room was palpable as he revealed his vision:

"This is where the Joy Force steps in. Imagine a world with three branches of the Joy Force—the Joy Force on Air, on Land, and on Sea—not warriors of destruction, but custodians of healing and positive transformation. Just as militaries stand ready to protect, Joy Force stands ready to uplift and serve."

The Joy Force in Action: Transformative Potential on Land, Air, and Sea

The audience sat spellbound as Manohara explained the transformative structure of each division. He painted an evocative picture of the power and potential of the Joy Force in its three branches:

"The Joy Force is more than a military—it is a movement for human dignity, compassion, and resilience. Imagine if every citizen felt defended not just from external threats but from the struggles of life itself, knowing that their protectors were also their healers, educators, and friends."

His concept transcended defense and reached into the heart of society, creating networks of hope, systems of support, and pathways of prosperity.

"Our youth, our sons and daughters, would become part of a force that is not measured by the battles it fights, but by the lives it touches. They would become not just soldiers, but pillars of peace and stability, guiding us toward a world of harmony."

The Joy Force as the Guiding Star of Abraham's Descendants

Turning back to the audience, Manohara raised his voice, filled with purpose:

"As descendants of Abraham, we are called to be a light unto the nations. The Joy Force is our way of fulfilling this divine calling. It is a force born of goodness, of universal love, and divine compassion—a gift to humanity, guiding all toward unity and peace."

The audience sat spellbound, enraptured by the beauty and promise of this vision. This was not just an idea; it was a calling to rise above the limitations of the past, to unite in the service of humanity, and to shine as Abraham's descendants were meant to shine—as stars guiding all of humanity.

An Unprecedented Force for Global Good

As he concluded, Manohara's words swelled with a climactic energy:

"The Joy Force is not just a proposal; it is an invitation to reshape the very nature of defense, to transform it into a force that embodies the highest values of our shared humanity. Imagine a world where armies defend dignity, where navies nurture life, and where air forces bring hope and healing."

Thunderous applause erupted, resonating through the hall like a clarion call to a new era. Manohara's vision, the Joy Force, was not just an idea; it was a beacon for a world that would look back on this day as the dawn of a new era, a movement rooted in compassion, unity, and the boundless potential of the human spirit.

The audience was moved, sensing the profoundness of this new reality. It was not just about protection; it was about creating a thriving, compassionate society. The Joy Force would stand as a **testament to the enduring legacy of Abraham's descendants,** as a light guiding the world into an era of peace, love, and unshakable joy.

The Dawn of a New Era: Joy Force on Land and Sea

The energy in the auditorium intensified as Manohara focused his gaze on the audience, an expression of sheer conviction on his face.

"Today, we live in a world where armies stand on the brink of conflict, equipped and trained for war. But I invite you to envision an army that doesn't only stand ready to engage in warfare but also to build, uplift, and empower communities. This is the transformative vision of the Joy Force on Land."

He spoke with a fervor that reached the depths of the audience's hearts.

"Imagine an army not focused on the tools of destruction but the tools of construction—an army devoted to creating, to healing, and to helping humanity thrive. The Joy Force on Land will be a powerful network of skilled engineers, compassionate medics, educators, and organizers, all united under a common purpose: the betterment of human life."

Manohara elaborated:

"These warriors would carry not rifles but equipment for progress. The engineering divisions within this force could erect bridges—not bridges meant for advancing into enemy territory, but ones that would unite divided communities. These bridges would be pathways to access, connection, and shared resources. They would connect villages that were previously isolated, bring healthcare to areas that had none, and carry educational resources to rural regions long neglected."

The **Joy Force on Land** would include **medical battalions** with an expanded mission, beyond tending to soldiers.

"They would be able to provide vaccines, perform surgeries, and even offer regular healthcare services in underserved regions," Manohara said.

"This is not just a relief army for times of crisis; it's an active presence, tending to the needs of society. It's about recognizing that every individual deserves access to health, safety, and opportunities to thrive. In drought-stricken areas, they could implement irrigation systems. In disaster-prone

regions, they could construct resilient housing."

Manohara described a **network that would be prepared to respond not only to natural disasters but to the everyday crises** that afflict impoverished areas globally:

"Imagine them creating sustainable agricultural practices, planting seeds of prosperity that nourish communities for generations. Under the Joy Force, this is not just an army—it's a network of hope, addressing the core issues of societal instability, such as lack of healthcare, education, and infrastructure. They would be true guardians of humanity's future."

The crowd was visibly moved by the **passion with which Manohara spoke of an army transformed from instruments of war into architects of progress,** builders of a better world.

The Joy Force at Sea: Empowering Coastal Communities and Bridging Nations

With the audience captivated, Manohara shifted to the next dimension of his vision.

"Now," he continued, **"let us turn our attention to the vast oceans and waterways that connect our continents, our lands, and our peoples. The Navy, traditionally a force of maritime power, projects strength across the seas. But what if we harnessed this strength not to dominate, but to support and sustain coastal communities? What if the Joy Force at Sea became a flotilla of hope, bringing resources, knowledge, and empowerment to the remotest corners of our coasts and islands?"**

The image was breathtaking. He described **ships not loaded with weapons but with seeds of growth and tools of education:**

"Imagine vessels setting sail with experts in environmental science, agriculture, healthcare, and socioeconomic development. Picture ships that carry agronomists who train communities in sustainable farming and fishing, equipping them to build resilient local economies."

His voice softened as he painted this vision:

"These ships wouldn't bear the insignia of war, but rather symbols of peace and prosperity. They would carry teams of doctors, agricultural specialists, and teachers—individuals who understand that the true strength of a community is in its ability to sustain and improve itself. They could travel to coastal regions, bringing tools for self-sustenance, delivering medical care, and educating youth in critical skills."

Joy Force as the Heartbeat of a New Nation

As he reached the culmination of his presentation, Manohara's voice echoed through the hall, vibrating with conviction:

"Brothers and sisters, the Joy Force is more than a concept. It is the heartbeat of a new kind of patriotism—a patriotism not bound by borders but by a profound respect for human life. It is a patriotism rooted not in the fear of the other, but in the celebration of our common humanity."

He explained that the **Joy Force wasn't intended to replace traditional defense but to stand alongside it**, complementing it with a spirit of service and compassion.

"This is not a force for conquest; it is a force for compassion. It is a way for our bravest citizens to channel their valor and courage into missions of healing, of uplifting, of transforming our world."

A Call to the Descendants of Abraham: Uniting Under the Joy Force

In a powerful declaration, Manohara addressed the assembly:

"Today, we stand as descendants of Abraham, called not to divide but to unite. The Joy Force is our mission to take the blessings given to Abraham and spread them across the Earth. Together, we will create a legacy of peace, joy, and interconnection that will shine across the ages. In a world so often divided, we will be the ones to build bridges and heal hearts."

Manohara introduced the concept of **Joy Force Training Centers**, places where young people from across the globe could gather to learn the arts of peacebuilding, community development, and joy ambassadorship. "Our youth will not be trained in the art of war, but in the art of joy. They will become ambassadors of hope, agents of change, unifiers of nations."

These centers would be the seedbeds of a generation dedicated not to conflict but to unity, compassion, and creative problem-solving. "Our young people," he said with pride, "will become the torchbearers of this vision, serving as beacons of peace in their communities, spreading the light of Abraham's legacy far and wide."

A Vision for a New World: The Dawn of the Joy Force
Manohara ended his presentation with a **powerful statement** that resonated deeply within the audience. **"The Joy Force is not merely an idea; it is a new path for humanity. It is a path illuminated by the divine light of peace that flows through each of us. This is a movement that will reshape the world—not by conquering lands, but by conquering hearts, by uniting us all in a shared purpose of upliftment, service, and joy."**

With these words, Manohara bid goodbye to the audience.

Thunderous applause filled the hall, a roar of affirmation and hope that reverberated through every corner of the room. People felt the weight of a new era dawning—a time when the **descendants of Abraham would not only shine as stars in the sky but would illuminate the Earth as beacons of love, peace, and joy.**

In that moment, everyone present knew that they were witnessing the **birth of something extraordinary. The Joy Force was not just a vision; it was a movement** to heal humanity, to lift the downtrodden, to break the chains of division, and to craft a future that reflected the **boundless goodness within every soul.** This was the Joy Force—**ready to transform the world, to build not just a nation, but an era where all of humanity could rise together, bound by the power of love and the unity of purpose.**

The dawn of the Joy Force had arrived, and with it, the promise of a new world.

Manjula Dev, the exuberant spokesperson, came on the digital screen. **"Hello again, my fellow descendants of Abraham, your eyes sparkle like the stars,"** she exclaimed!

"The message of the conclave is crystal clear," she said. "Let us consciously and constantly keep focusing on the unifying and shared common aspects of peace, joy, and purpose. Then we, the descendants of Abraham, can build a legacy that will transcend historical and theological divides."

"The spirituality of peace and joy is our shared heritage, a boundless legacy," she stated. "It transcends every difference and calls us into a realm where **love is the highest law."**

Emphasizing that this **vision of Abrahamic harmony is not only attainable but already present,** awaiting only humanity's collective willingness to embrace it fully, she said, **"Let us constantly remind ourselves that the unity of Abraham's descendants is both a spiritual inheritance and a collective responsibility, guiding us toward a future of harmony, mutual respect, and shared joy."**

She went on to emphasize both the **complexity and the necessity of building bridges across religious divides.** "This endeavor presents a unique **opportunity for transformation, encouraging Muslims, Christians, Jews, and everyone else to transcend past old enmities and embrace a shared joyful future,"** Manjula inspired and motivated the audience.

"By grounding our actions in love, mutual respect, and compassion, pursuing the common mission of joy for all, we, the descendants of Abraham, can create a future that is inclusive, equitable, and enduring," Manjula emphatically stated.

Building on this energy that was enveloping the participants, Manjula exhorted the Yeshuans to go beyond mere tolerance. **"We are called for reimagining relationships between us, elevating our consciousness, to see beyond labels, and to recognize love as the foundation upon which true peace is built.** A call to build a world that reflects the divine light within each of us," Manjula declared.

Ultimately, the **Yeshuan vision is one of boundless potential, a vision in which humanity's greatest achievements lie not in conquest or dominance, but in unity and love.** Through this lens, the **future of the descendants of Abraham is not only filled with hope but brimming with the possibility of a world that embodies the joy, peace, and oneness that is humanity's shared spiritual inheritance.**

CHAPTER 19

The Heavenly Assembly with Questions

The **celestial realm thrummed with anticipation** as the Angels gathered, filling the heavens with their radiant forms, their very beings reflecting the glory of their Creator. Created higher than human beings but beneath the transcendent majesty of Yeshua, the resurrected King, these divine beings had long served as God's messengers and guardians. They were the protectors, defenders, and emissaries of God's will. Yet today, as they looked down upon Earth, a new awe filled their spirits—a stirring within, a kindling of joy, and, for some, a lingering question that had long ached within their hearts.

The Angels had borne witness to the **suffering, courage, and resilience of humanity for eons**, interceding for Earth and carrying out their divine duties with unwavering loyalty. But today, the extraordinary was unfolding below—a historic event that shifted the very fabric of Heaven and Earth. It was the global virtual conclave of the Yeshuans, a sacred gathering uniting the descendants of Abraham in purpose, healing, and joy. This assembly marked an unparalleled moment in history, a time when the promises of God were coming alive in unprecedented unity.

The Divine Gathering of the Yeshuans

The Angels watched intently as the conclave unfolded—a sacred spectacle of **declarations of peace, unity, and shared purpose among the descendants of Abraham**. They saw the path of harmony the descendants of Abraham were being led to—a reflection of God's love, His intricate plan, finally revealed in beauty and completeness. This was a moment Heaven had anticipated for ages—a moment of reconciliation where the divisions of time, land, and belief were momentarily erased. It was the dawn of a new age, and as the Angels bore witness, many wept tears of joy, their praise rising softly through the heavens.

Yet, amid the praise, a faint murmur began to ripple across the heavenly assembly, a question voiced by one young Angel who trembled with sorrow.

"Why now, only now?" he asked, his voice tinged with a grief as old as creation itself. **"Couldn't this unity have come sooner? Why did it take centuries of suffering, war, and loss to bring about this harmony? We have**

watched children weep, the innocent fall, and families torn apart. Couldn't this peace have come to Earth before so much sorrow?"

A Cry for Understanding: The Memory of Lucifer

As the Angels contemplated this question, another memory stirred within them—a memory of one of their own, one who had once held a beauty and brilliance that rivaled the brightest stars.

Lucifer, the "Light Bearer," had once been the most magnificent of all, adorned with wisdom and beauty that reflected God's own glory. Created with a purpose as profound as light itself, Lucifer's radiance was intended to uplift, to illuminate, and to serve. But within him, pride began to take root—a pride that would grow into a rebellion, reverberating across the heavens and shaping the destiny of angelic and human realms alike.

Lucifer's heart became consumed by **self-reflection and ambition**. He, who had once mirrored the light of his Creator, grew enamored with his own brilliance. He desired power beyond his purpose, aspiring not just to reflect light but to be worshipped as the source of it. Driven by pride, he stirred dissent among the angels, casting shadows where there had only been light. In his rebellion, he sought to claim dominion, gathering a host of followers, and their clash with Heaven's loyal forces became the first war—a war that led to his fall and forever altered the divine order.

The consequences of Lucifer's fall were devastating. **He who had been called to illuminate had become the Prince of Darkness,** and in his fall, he sowed the seeds of pride, envy, and conflict that would touch not only the angelic realms but humanity as well. Since that time, the Angels had carried the memory of Lucifer's rebellion, a stark reminder of the dangers of pride and the importance of humility, loyalty, and love. As they watched humanity struggle with the same shadows, they longed to see Earth embrace the light that Lucifer had once forsaken.

The Question of Suffering: A Search for Divine Wisdom

The Angels' murmurs grew, not of rebellion but of sincere questioning—a longing for understanding. They struggled with the pain of witnessing humanity's suffering, a sorrow that resonated with their ancient memory of loss.

As their voices rose, the **Archangel Michael**, majestic and calm, stepped forward. His presence commanded reverence, and with a single gaze, he quieted the assembly.

"My dear fellow Angels," he began, his voice a balm to their questioning hearts, **"it is not for us to question the depths of God's will. He alone is the Author of life and death, the Master of time and destiny. What we witness, though painful, unfolds with a purpose that far exceeds our understanding. Yes, humanity has endured unimaginable suffering, but remember that much of this pain has stemmed from choices made out of pride, anger, and fear—the very traits that brought Lucifer down."**

Michael's words resonated through the assembly, a reminder of the eternal struggle between light and darkness.

"From the moment of Lucifer's rebellion, the choice between pride and humility, self-glory and service, has been laid before every soul. Even in their darkness, God's love has shone through humanity's trials, guiding, forgiving, and redeeming. This conclave, this unprecedented unity among Abraham's descendants, is a testimony to God's enduring mercy. Every intercession, every prayer we have lifted for Earth, has been heard. This gathering is the fruit of our efforts, a beacon of hope born from centuries of divine patience and endless love."

A New Covenant of Joy: The Angels' Renewed Purpose

Humbled and inspired, the Angels felt their hearts swell with understanding. Their questioning spirits found peace in Michael's wisdom, seeing that they, too, played a part in the intricate tapestry of God's plan. This moment on Earth, this bridging of Heaven and humanity, was not an end but a beginning—a chance for humanity to rise from the ashes of pride and conflict and to embrace the unity and joy for which they were created.

Michael's voice rose once more, resonating with authority and compassion.

"The time for redemption is now. The door is open, and Earth's inhabitants are answering the call to love, to unity, to joy. Let us renew our devotion and intercede with greater fervor, lifting every soul that reaches out toward the light. Let us praise God, for He is worthy of all exaltation and honor!"

The Song of the Angels: A New Covenant of Joy

Their song filled the heavens, a powerful wave of adoration that acknowledged the story of Lucifer's fall and celebrated God's unending grace. The Angels glorified God, exalting His perfect timing, His unending compassion, and His power to transform even the darkest circumstances into a legacy of peace and joy.

With one voice, they proclaimed:

"Blessed be the Great I AM, the Creator of all, the One who binds humanity with threads of love and light. All praise to the God who redeems and restores, who brings forth unity and peace!"

The Joy of Harmony: Heaven's New Dawn

The **Angels knew that this conclave was more than just a gathering**; it was the dawn of a new era. It was a call for humanity to rise above division and hatred, to reach for God's light with open hearts. And they, the Angels, would stand as protectors, as intercessors, as guardians of this new unity, this covenant of joy.

Michael looked upon them, his spirit renewed, and declared:

"We are called not just to witness, but to support and sustain this vision. Let our intercessions be unceasing. Let our prayers pour out like rivers, lifting humanity to God's grace."

The Angels resumed their eternal mission, not as mere witnesses but as **active participants in a divine plan that would lift the world from darkness to light, from suffering to joy**.

Their **voices filled the heavens once more**, a symphony of love and joy that celebrated the Creator—the Great I AM. The Angels, now united in a purpose as deep as the ages and as boundless as the universe, proclaimed:

"All glory to the Creator, the Source of life, the Fountain of joy, the One who calls all into unity and peace."

SECTION E: ANSWERING QUERIES FROM THE CONCLAVE

Following the global virtual summit organized by the Yeshuans, where Yaseva, the convenor, spoke about the "Nine-fold Descendants of Abraham," the message generated significant interest and stirred thoughtful responses. His vision of unity, rooted in a shared Abrahamic heritage, was meant to inspire cooperation, healing, and peace among historically divided communities. However, questions soon emerged, probing the feasibility of such a vision in today's world—particularly given the entrenched conflicts, economic interests, and mistrust that persist. While some dismissed the vision as idealistic, others raised constructive inquiries aimed at understanding the real-world challenges to unity.

CHAPTER 20

Query on Jewish and Christian Investments in the Armament Industry

One of the most pressing issues raised involved the **substantial investments from Jewish and Christian sources in the armament industry**—a sector largely seen as contrary to the vision of peace and cooperation. Some participants questioned whether this financial entanglement with defense and weapon manufacturing might hinder the journey toward reconciliation. Specifically, they asked whether those profiting from armaments would willingly shift their resources toward investments that align more closely with the mission of peace.

Yaseva acknowledged these concerns, noting that the influence of the armament industry among both Jewish and Christian investors is indeed significant. This influence, he explained, goes beyond personal wealth to **shaping national policies and perpetuating militaristic ideologies.** He emphasized that any meaningful progress toward unity would require a **realignment of values—prioritizing social investments that nurture life over industries that rely on conflict.**

Being a **Joypreneur** at heart, Yaseva took the opportunity to explore the **scope and pragmatic opportunities to repurpose the investment of the 'Descendants of Abraham' in Armament Companies,** which surely would not be an act pleasing to God. Prominent figures and companies involved in the armament sector within both Jewish and Christian circles underscore the **challenge and potential for transformation.**

Notable Jewish Investors and Companies in the Armament Industry

Throughout history, several Jewish individuals and families have been associated with the armament industry, their investments spanning from the early 19th century to the modern era. Historically, figures and organizations such as **Samuel Colt, Nathan Mayer Rothschild, Elbit Systems, Israel Aerospace, and Rafael Advanced Defense Systems** contributed to the development and supply of arms, shaping the industry across Europe and beyond.

In modern times, **Israeli companies and investors have expanded this influence,** particularly as Israel has developed into a prominent center for defense technology.

Yaseva agreed that, while lucrative, these investments pose a challenge for initiatives promoting Abrahamic harmony. Profits generated by these industries often fund political stances that are at odds with peace, creating a complex web of interests that would need restructuring to align with a vision of Abrahamic harmony.

Christian Investors and Companies in the Armament Industry

Several attendees highlighted a **striking paradox:** while Christians are called by Christ to be peacemakers, many in the Christian community are heavily invested in the armament industry, especially in the United States.

Some participants questioned whether Christian investors could move away from manufacturing and profiting from weapons—a business that fuels conflict and stands in stark contrast to the message of peace and love espoused by Christ.

Yaseva acknowledged this valid concern, noting the significant Christian involvement in the armament sector, which has become publicly visible and, at times, controversial. **"It is unfortunate," Yaseva said, "that those who profess to follow Christ find themselves invested in industries that contradict the values of love, peace, and joy."**

Prominent Christian figures and organizations have longstanding ties to the defense industry. Notable examples include:

- **Richard DeVos**: Co-founder of Amway, a significant investor in defense contracts.
- **Erik Prince**: Founder of Blackwater Worldwide, known for its private military services, with a background influenced by Christian ideologies.
- **General Dynamics**: Originally founded by John Philip Holland, an Irish-American Catholic, it is now a leading U.S. defense contractor.
- **Lockheed Martin**: One of the largest U.S. defense contractors, with several Christian-affiliated investors.
- **Raytheon Technologies**: Founded by Vannevar Bush, a Methodist, Raytheon remains a powerful player in the defense industry.

- **BAE Systems**: A U.K.-based contractor with close connections to Christian investors, one of the largest arms suppliers globally.
- **The Vatican's Investment Portfolio**: Estimated at $500M-$1B in defense industries, the Vatican has faced scrutiny over its defense investments.
- **The Church of England's Investment Fund**: Holds investments in various defense contractors.
- **The Presbyterian Church (USA)'s Investment Fund**: Includes holdings in the defense sector.

Moving Forward: A Call to Realign Investments with Peaceful Progress

The question remains: **Can these historically rooted investments in the armament industry pivot toward peaceful ventures that benefit all of humanity?**

Yaseva proposed that both Jewish and Christian communities consider how their economic influence might be **re-channeled into industries that build life, infrastructure, and sustainability rather than those that rely on conflict.**

By shifting toward investments in **education, healthcare, clean energy, and sustainable agriculture,** the descendants of Abraham could create a lasting impact that echoes their shared values.

"This transformation would not be immediate, and resistance would undoubtedly arise," Yaseva acknowledged. **"However, the potential for creating a unified legacy of compassion, healing, and constructive collaboration is immense."**

A Vision for Peaceful Investment: The Path to Abrahamic Harmony

He expressed a hope that Christians could **gradually shift away from profiting from weapons** and instead consider industries that promote the **welfare and growth of society**—sectors that align with **values central to the kingdom of God.**

The Path to Abrahamic Harmony Through Sustainable Investment

The global virtual summit underscored the **importance of examining how economic power can support or hinder unity among Abraham's descendants.** The presence of **influential Jewish and Christian investors in the armament**

sector reveals an entrenched dependency on defense as a source of wealth and security. Nevertheless, if these resources were redirected, the results could be transformative.

Yaseva emphasized that by investing in fields that **enrich communities—rather than destabilize them—both Jewish and Christian leaders can make strides toward achieving the harmonious vision of Abraham's descendants.** The legacy of Abraham would then be a testament to shared peace, rather than shared conflict, illuminating a path forward that honors the richness of their faiths while uplifting all humanity.

In this light, the challenge extends beyond faith and tradition to an **urgent call for the descendants of Abraham to turn their collective power toward constructing a future** that promotes **sustainable peace and shared prosperity.**

Redirecting Investments Toward Sustainable Industries

Yaseva pointed out that the world's resources and attention are pivotal to ethical and sustainable development. The opportunity to invest in industries that serve humanity has never been greater. He emphasized that **Christian investors, as well as those from other faith communities,** have the option to contribute to **industries that support global needs.**

Investing in **peace-promoting fields** like renewable energy, sustainable agriculture, healthcare, biotechnology, and education technology would not only align with Christian values but would also provide **substantial returns and long-term societal impact.**

To illustrate a way forward, a team member suggested the following **Peaceful Industries for Ethical Investment:**

* **Renewable Energy**: Solar, wind, and hydro energy investments help reduce dependence on fossil fuels and contribute to a sustainable future.
* **Sustainable Agriculture**: Supporting innovative farming methods protects resources and ensures food security.
* **Healthcare and Biotechnology**: Investments in medical technology improve quality of life and bring healthcare advancements to underserved communities.
* **Education Technology**: Funding accessible education tools benefits society by empowering individuals and communities.

- **Environmental Conservation**: Investing in conservation initiatives directly combats climate change and preserves the Earth for future generations.

Shifting to Investments That Foster Harmony and Growth

The **descendants of Abraham** have the option to **support economic ventures that align with principles of justice, peace, and joy.** This shift not only offers ethical and spiritual benefits but also the opportunity for the descendants of Abraham to position themselves as **leaders in a socially responsible investment landscape.**

Supporting industries and embracing Socially Responsible Investing (SRI), particularly focusing on **ethical funds, microfinance, and social entrepreneurship,** would mark a significant step forward.

Typical Socially Responsible Investment Opportunities include:

- **Impact Investing**: Directing capital to ventures that generate positive social and environmental impact.
- **Ethical Funds**: Mutual funds that avoid businesses linked to harmful practices, including armaments and environmentally damaging operations.
- **Community Development Financial Institutions (CDFIs)**: Financing community development initiatives, often supporting underserved regions.
- **Microfinance**: Providing small loans to individuals in developing areas, enabling them to build sustainable livelihoods.
- **Social Entrepreneurship**: Supporting businesses that prioritize social impact over profit maximization.

Jewish and Israeli Companies Leading the Shift

Yaseva acknowledged the growing interest in value-driven investing, with organizations and funds that promote **ethical investments.** The global community can take inspiration from **Israeli companies** making strides in renewable energy, healthcare, and autonomous vehicle technology—sectors that prioritize **sustainability and global well-being.**

Examples of **Israeli Companies Pioneering Ethical Investments include:**

- **Ormat Technologies (Renewable Energy)**: Developing clean energy solutions to reduce environmental impact.
- **SodaStream (Sustainable Consumer Products)**: Providing alternatives to single-use plastics.
- **Teva Pharmaceutical Industries (Healthcare)**: Advancing affordable healthcare and medications.
- **Babylon Health (Digital Healthcare)**: Enhancing access to healthcare through digital platforms.
- **Innoviz Technologies (Autonomous Vehicles)**: Pioneering safer, smarter transportation.

Additionally, there are **Jewish funds focusing on ethical and social impact investing, aligning with values like Tikkun Olam (repairing the world):**

- **Tikkun Olam Impact Fund**
- **Jewish Values Investment Fund**
- **The Abraham Fund Initiatives**
- **Jewish Community Investment Fund**
- **UJA-Federation of New York's Impact Investing**

Embracing a New Economic Paradigm for Unity

Yaseva emphasized that the path forward lies in **harmonizing investments with ethical and spiritual principles,** thereby cultivating an economy that reflects the aspirations of a **united Abrahamic family.** Such a transformation would create an **economic system built on justice, compassion, and global sustainability.**

This approach calls all communities, especially the Christian and Jewish communities, to **transcend the profit-at-all-cost mentality** and instead invest in building a **sustainable, just, and harmonious world.**

As a **call to action**, Yaseva reminded attendees that **economic resources and investments are extensions of spiritual values.** By **channeling resources toward peaceful, ethical, and sustainable ventures,** all descendants of Abraham have the opportunity to exemplify **love, peace, and joy.** This realignment could serve as a **powerful bridge across divides,** uniting the Abrahamic family in shared responsibility for a brighter future.

The questions raised at the Yeshuan summit served as an **important reminder that true unity goes beyond words; it demands actions** that reflect **mutual respect, understanding, and compassion.** In prioritizing **investments that foster peace and social progress,** the descendants of Abraham can indeed move towards a world where the **legacy of their shared ancestor is honored—not through divisions or conflict, but through a commitment to uplifting all of humanity.**

CHAPTER 21

Query on the Sunni-Shia Divide in light of Abrahamic harmony

The recent Yeshuan global summit unveiled a **visionary goal**—the ninefold descendants of Abraham standing united, transcending millennia of theological and historical divides. This ambitious concept resonated with many and sparked excitement, yet it also raised crucial questions from attendees, particularly those from the Islamic community. They questioned the feasibility of unity amid deep-rooted divisions, with the **Sunni-Shia schism** emerging as a key focal point. This topic not only highlighted hopes for reconciliation but also shed light on the considerable challenges involved in healing these ancient divides.

The Sunni-Shia Divide: A Complex Web of History, Theology, and Geopolitics

A question from the summit's participants delved into the obstacles that persist in **Sunni-Shia unity**, particularly in regions with complex relationships, such as Iraq and Iran. The **Sunni-Shia split** is rooted in historical events following the death of the Prophet Muhammad, leading to differing beliefs regarding leadership succession. However, this religious divide has since evolved into a **multifaceted and often politicized conflict** that influences economic, political, and social landscapes globally.

This schism is not only theological; it includes **territorial disputes**, differing regional interests, and international power plays. Additionally, the presence of valuable resources, such as **oil in the Middle East**, adds to the economic tension and escalates competition between predominantly Sunni and Shia states.

Yaseva's Response: Learning from the Protestant-Catholic Divide

Yaseva, convenor of the Yeshuan movement, addressed this pressing question by offering insights rooted in **historical parallels** and a **vision of unity**, underscoring the Yeshuan mission to bridge all Abrahamic divides. He offered an **analogy drawn from Christianity's historical rifts**, specifically between Protestantism and Catholicism, a division that once plunged Europe into wars and political upheaval.

"There was a time," Yaseva remarked, **"when Protestants and Catholics fought wars, spilled blood, and tore societies apart due to theological and territorial disputes."** Despite this, the Christian world eventually moved beyond those divides. He highlighted that, in the modern era, **Catholics and Protestants coexist peacefully and respectfully across the globe**, collaborating in many shared causes and humanitarian missions.

He then invited **Muslim sects** to imagine a similar healing of divisions within Islam. Both Sunni and Shia sects, he noted, share a **deep reverence for the Prophet Muhammad and the teachings of the Quran.**"Both traditions declare 'Allah Akbar'—God is great," he emphasized, pointing to a shared foundation upon which unity could be built. Through this prism, he urged both groups to **transcend their differences** and come together with **mutual respect and compassion.**

A Higher Perspective: Shifting from Division to a Shared Humanity

In answering this query, **Yaseva called on the Islamic people** to consider a universal approach focused on the **welfare of humanity as a whole.**"Allah is the God of all people," he said, **"and His grace and mercy extend to everyone, not solely one sect over another."** He emphasized that the God revered by both Sunni and Shia Muslims is a **God of compassion**, who beckons believers to treat others with love and mercy.

Such a vision does not merely aim for tolerance; it calls for **active collaboration and understanding across cultural and religious lines.** By fostering mutual respect, both Sunni and Shia Muslims—and indeed all Abrahamic faith traditions—can work towards **collective goals that transcend sectarianism.** This unified mission includes the pursuit of peace, the cultivation of joy, and the fostering of global harmony. These are values that **resonate across faiths and cultures**, forming the foundation of a **united Abrahamic legacy** that connects individuals and communities around the globe.

A Spiritual Approach to Moving Beyond Sectarianism

Yaseva urged transcending these divides, advocating for an **overcoming and deeper spiritual shift** centered on the values of **joy and peace.** He underscored that the path to **true unity lies in embracing the power of love**—a love that sees beyond labels and differences to **embrace all of humanity as part of the family of Abraham**. This view invites followers of **Islam, Christianity, and Judaism** to recognize that, while religious practices and beliefs may differ, these distinctions should not hinder **respect, empathy, or cooperation**.

"Whether one is Shia or Sunni, Catholic or Protestant, each seeks peace and joy in their lives," Yaseva explained, underscoring that **love is the force capable of guiding people to these aspirations**. This love is a **"universal bridge,"** connecting people regardless of faith or background, and enabling them to focus on **shared values**. By practicing such **"unconditional love,"** the descendants of Abraham can foster a world where **trust and mutual respect replace rivalry and division**.

Addressing Geopolitical and Economic Pressures in Pursuit of Spiritual Unity

Yaseva cautioned that the divide between Sunni and Shia Islam is further complicated and manipulated by **geopolitical forces**, including the influence of **superpowers** and the **regional politics surrounding oil and other resources**. He acknowledged these **real-world challenges**, noting that international economic and political pressures often exacerbate religious divides. However, he expressed confidence that such pressures can be **overwhelmed by the pragmatic pursuit of a peaceful, joyful, and meaningful life**.

"All descendants of Abraham—Muslims, Christians, Jews, and all those who follow the path of love, need to focus on channelling their energies into building a future marked by respect, compassion, and the pursuit of joy," Yaseva said. This requires **difficult yet necessary choices**, such as prioritizing **spiritual growth over material gain**, promoting **peace over political dominance**, and choosing **cooperation over rivalry**.

For Sunni and Shia Muslims, this means **imagining a world where sectarian identities are acknowledged but do not restrict one's contributions to humanity**.

The **path forward calls for a transformation in mindset**, where unity is not viewed as the abandonment of cultural or religious identity but as an **embrace of shared values. Yaseva encouraged all descendants of Abraham to prioritize spiritual unity** over geopolitical and economic concerns. While these factors may add complexity to relations between countries, the **true path forward requires both humility and courage—humility** to respect differences and **courage** to place the welfare of all people above narrow self-interest.

This **higher purpose** transcends temporary challenges, inviting all descendants of Abraham to a **greater calling rooted in compassion, integrity, and hope.**

The Zionist Expansionists

Another critical question raised by some of the Conclave attendees was about the **Zionist expansionist agenda** and whether its momentum could realistically be tempered in pursuit of harmony. Many viewed the Zionist movement, rooted in a **historical response to persecution,** as a complex blend of **cultural identity, survival, and national defense.** The movement often ties itself to **ancient scriptures,** claiming a divinely ordained right to the land, which complicates peace initiatives.

Yaseva addressed this with compassion, noting that the historical persecution faced by **Jewish communities worldwide** has undoubtedly contributed to the **fervor with which Zionism is pursued today.** The intense need for security has been **magnified by generational trauma,** leading to actions that sometimes escalate rather than resolve tensions. He encouraged a shift toward the **joy and fulfillment that comes from creating harmony rather than expanding borders**—a joy that cannot be obtained by taking from others.

To build trust, **Yaseva stressed, Jewish communities must consider a path that genuinely values the well-being and dignity of all people,** including their neighbors. Only by moving beyond **land acquisition toward true partnership** can they experience the deeper joy that peace and shared purpose bring.

Blind Support for Dogmatic Scriptural Stances

Another significant point raised by attendees was the **Christian community's tendency to unconditionally support Israel,** even in controversial and hostile actions against Palestine. **Yaseva addressed this, saying, "While Christians are encouraged to pray for Israel, this does not imply that every action by the state of Israel is morally justified."**

He urged Christians to consider the **implications of such one-sided support,** which often overlooks the **realities faced by displaced Palestinians** and the complexities of the **Middle East conflict.**

Yaseva's response called for a balanced approach, one that supports **justice and advocates for peace for all parties involved.** By engaging with **empathy and respect for all descendants of Abraham,** he suggested, Christians could foster a **more inclusive path toward peace**—one that does not **idolize any state or authority** but instead seeks **true harmony.**

CHAPTER 22

Spirituality of Hinduism Sects in Abrahamic Descendants

At the **Yeshuan global summit**, a profound vision was presented—a call for **unity among the ninefold descendants of Abraham** that transcends historical, theological, and cultural divides. The summit's message was warmly received, bringing participants together in a shared aspiration for **peace and harmony.** A notable group of **Hindu representatives**, particularly the followers of **Saivite and Vaishnavite traditions** from South India's Tamil community, expressed their **thrill and pleasant surprise** at how their ancient spiritual heritage **resonated with the Yeshuan framework of love, harmony, and joy.** They highlighted the shared values and distinctions between Hindu spirituality and the Abrahamic vision, offering insights into how diverse traditions can find **common ground.**

The Role of the Vedic Tradition: Why Was It Not Included?

A significant question posed by some **Brahmin sect Hindu attendees** was about the **exclusion of Vedic followers** from the ninefold descendants of Abraham's vision. The **Vedic texts—Rig, Yajur, Sama, and Atharva—are foundational to Hinduism**, so why were these traditions not included in this unifying vision of love?

Yaseva, the convenor of the Yeshuan movement, responded by explaining that the **Vedas**, while sacred, are primarily oriented toward **reverence for nature**, with the **Rig Veda** in particular celebrating natural elements like the **sun, fire, and water.** These texts originated in **ancient oral traditions** brought by Indo-Iranian migrants and carried forward by **early Persian priests** who practiced **fire worship.** This nature-centered spirituality, though foundational, is distinct from the **love-based Abrahamic vision** promoted by the Yeshuan movement.

Yaseva emphasized that the Yeshuan vision seeks to include traditions focused on **universal, all-embracing love**, aligning more closely with the **Saivite and Vaishnavite teachings** than with the **Vedic approach to nature worship.** However, he clarified that **any follower, regardless of their adherence to the Vedas**, who embodies **love in their heart is already aligned with the Yeshuan ideals.** Unity, he explained, transcends specific doctrines and flows from a **heart committed to love and compassion.**

Understanding Hindu Iconography and the Place of Idols in Spiritual Life

Another significant question from Hindu attendees addressed the **practice of idol worship.** Hinduism is renowned for its **elaborate iconography**, with idols and images of gods and goddesses representing a **wide spectrum of spiritual attributes.** This visible aspect of Hinduism—its **colorful idols, expressive figurines, and detailed temple carvings**—is often perceived as at odds with the **Yeshuan movement's focus on an inner, love-based spirituality.**

Yaseva explained that Hindu idols are best understood as **symbolic representations of divine qualities** rather than literal gods. Figures like **Durga, Kali, Lakshmi, and Saraswati** represent specific aspects of life: **Durga embodies strength, Kali represents protection, Lakshmi signifies abundance,** and **Saraswati is associated with wisdom.** These idols serve as **guides and reminders of divine attributes** rather than objects of direct worship.

In **Saivism and Vaishnavism**, which emphasize **divine love as the ultimate truth**, idols serve as **visual aids** to focus devotion and reverence, but the ultimate goal remains **internal—realizing love within oneself.** The Yeshuan vision does not exclude practices that use imagery, provided they point back to the **essential truth that love is at the core of spirituality.** This perspective encourages Hindu followers to see the divine essence as residing within all beings, recognizing that the visible idols are reflections of the invisible love and divinity that connects all.

Saivism and Vaishnavism: Love as the Central Tenet of Faith

One of the summit's most powerful discussions was the shared foundation of **love in Saivism and Vaishnavism**, two major Hindu traditions originating in Tamil Nadu. The saying, **"Anbe Sivam"—"Love is Shiva"**, epitomizes the Saivite understanding that **God is not only a distant deity but the embodiment of love itself.** Similarly, **Vaishnavism** places a deep emphasis on **devotion (bhakti)** and **compassionate service.**

Historically, **Saivism and Vaishnavism** have spread the message that **love is central to spirituality.** This belief was further popularized in Tamil Nadu by **early Christian influences**, including the **Apostle Thomas**, who, according to tradition, brought the **teachings of divine love** to the region. These teachings emphasized **peace, compassion, and unity**—values that strongly resonate with the **Yeshuan call for a universal family united by love.**

In this context, followers of Saivism and Vaishnavism are naturally aligned with the Yeshuan vision of an Abrahamic family united by love. The Yeshuan movement thus sees these traditions as integral parts of the global spiritual community, where each tradition brings its own unique contributions while embracing the common foundation of love.

Reconciling the Northern and Southern Depictions of Shiva

An insightful question highlighted the **differing depictions of Shiva** in North and South India. In the South, Shiva is typically portrayed as a **god of love and compassion**, while in Northern India, he is often seen as a **fierce deity associated with destruction.** This regional variation raises an important question: How do these differing images align with the Yeshuan emphasis on a loving and compassionate God?

Yaseva explained that historical and cultural factors have influenced Shiva's portrayal in different regions. In Northern India, the **warrior classes and ruling elites** reshaped Shiva's image to reflect **strength, power, and conquest**, resonating with the **military values** of their societies. In contrast, in South India, Shiva is traditionally seen as a **deity of peace, compassion, and inner transformation**—qualities that align more closely with the **Yeshuan vision.**

Yaseva emphasized that how one views the divine can shape their character. A **God of love fosters love and compassion**, while a **god of anger and destruction can inspire divisive attitudes.**

Integrating Hinduism's Rich Symbolism into a Unified Vision of Love

The summit's discussions made it clear that Hinduism's diverse spiritual expressions—its idols, its deities, its regional variations—are all forms of connecting with the divine from primordial times. However, the common thread of refined, contemporary spirituality is evident in Saivism and Vaishnavism sects of Hindu religion, that are based on the belief that divine love permeates all of existence. This understanding allows these Hindu followers to participate fully in the Yeshuan vision without compromising their own traditions.

In this broader context, Hinduism's iconic symbols can be seen as representations of qualities that support unity and compassion. For instance, the multiple forms of the goddess reflect the nurturing, protective, and wise aspects of divinity, encouraging followers to embody these qualities in their own lives. The myriad representations within the Hindu religions of Saivism and Vaishnavism ,ultimately converge on the same truth that the Yeshuan vision espouses: love is the universal force that binds all beings.

Moving Forward: Hindu Participation in the Yeshuan Vision

For Hindus, particularly those practicing **Saivism and Vaishnavism**, the **Yeshuan vision** presents an invitation to engage with a **global community rooted in love, respect, and unity.** The movement encourages all who embrace love to consider themselves part of a **larger family**, where spirituality transcends labels and is defined by **compassion, selflessness, and a commitment to peace.**

The **Abrahamic vision** does not demand adherence to specific rituals or doctrines. Instead, it calls for an **inner alignment with love and kindness,** values central to Hindu spirituality. This perspective invites Hindu followers to honor their traditions while recognizing that they share a **common spiritual heritage** with people of all faiths. By fostering this inclusive approach, the Yeshuan movement aims to build a world where love unites rather than divides.

Conclusion: Embracing a Shared Spiritual Heritage of Love and Compassion

The questions raised by **Hindu participants** at the Yeshuan Conclave underscore a profound truth: **spirituality, at its core, is a journey toward love and unity.** The diverse practices and beliefs within Hinduism, especially those centered on love in **Saivism and Vaishnavism,** demonstrate that these traditions are naturally aligned with the **Abrahamic vision of a family united by compassion.**

The Yeshuan summit's message offers a new way of seeing **religious diversity—not as separate paths but as branches of the same tree rooted in love.** Through this lens, all spiritual traditions, including Hinduism, can find a place within the **greater family of Abraham,** united by the shared desire for **peace, joy, and mutual respect.**

In **Yaseva's words, "If love fills your heart, you are already a part of this fold, a Yeshuan, and a shining star in the heritage of Abraham."**

By focusing on this **common foundation**, the Yeshuan vision invites **Hindus and people of all faiths** to transcend divisions and contribute to a world where **love, understanding, and harmony** are paramount. This inclusive perspective holds the **promise of a future** where all people, regardless of background, can work together to create a **global community rooted in the timeless values of compassion, unity, and peace.**

SECTION F - "OPERATION DOUBLE PORTION: RESTORATION AND REJUVENATION OF ABRAHAMIC DESCENDANTS"

CHAPTER 23

Operation Double Portion:

An Initiative for Peace and Restoration for Israeli and Palestinian Families

For many years, **Yaseva** had nurtured an initiative titled **"Double Portion"** to lend a helping hand to the youth, mothers and their children, and other vulnerable groups struggling in conflict-torn regions such as **Palestine, Israel, Lebanon**, and other parts of the Middle East. **Inflation and economic hardship** are so severe that even **Israeli youth** find it difficult to marry and establish a home. Meanwhile, in war zones like Gaza, **Palestinians face unimaginable hardship**, with innocent lives continually sacrificed at the altar of heartless Zionist policies.

In these appointed times, **Yaseva** presented a comprehensive proposal on behalf of the **Yeshuans** and the cause of the **Descendants of Abraham**, aiming to please the **God of Compassion**. This mission sought to provide **new life and hope to children living in Middle Eastern war zones**, restoring a semblance of normalcy to their childhoods.

Particularly under the **Zionist government** in Israel, whose **cold-hearted policies** disregard justice and the plight of those they seek to displace—a gross violation of Yahweh's commandments—this mission has become even more urgent.

Yaseva entrusted this proposal to his close friend and co-worker, **Dr. Peter Ignatius**, Principal of the **Lakeview Bible Centre** on the outskirts of Chennai, India. Dr. Ignatius, a committed Yeshuan, received the proposal, which is outlined below.

Double Portion Mission Statement

"Descendants of Abraham, united by faith and compassion, extend a helping hand to traumatized Israeli and Palestinian families. Operation Double Portion provides a safe haven in supportive global communities, promoting peace, understanding, and selfless love."

Operation Double Portion emerges as a profound humanitarian mission to address the deep-seated trauma and displacement experienced by Israeli and Palestinian families. By offering refuge, support, and a pathway toward cultural integration, this initiative seeks to go beyond temporary relief, embodying a commitment to lasting peace and reconciliation. This ambitious project represents not only a direct response to the impacts of a historic conflict but also an innovative model for fostering global compassion, unity, and healing across cultural and faith lines.

Objectives of Operation Double Portion

The mission's objectives are built on a foundation of **empathy, unity, and resilience**, including:

- **Provide Refuge and Sanctuary**: Create a safe and nurturing environment for approximately **1,000 displaced families** within the first year.
- **Establish a Network of Host Families and Communities**: Mobilize **host families globally** to ensure integration and acceptance for affected families.
- **Facilitate Cultural Integration and Language Support**: Offer **language training, cross-cultural education,** and support programs fostering seamless integration into host societies.
- **Provide Psychological Support and Trauma Counseling**: Equip families with **trauma counseling and specialized emotional support**, especially for children.
- **Promote Dialogue, Reconciliation, and Healing**: Encourage **meaningful exchanges** to foster empathy, understanding, and a shared vision of peace among diverse families.

Project Vision: Compassion and Empathy at the Core

Operation Double Portion responds to the **severe humanitarian needs** resulting from the Israeli-Palestinian conflict. It focuses on the **human experience**—the mothers, fathers, and children impacted by displacement, loss, and violence. By addressing **immediate needs and long-term integration**, the initiative offers a pathway to **healing, stability, and renewed hope**.

Promoting Interfaith Unity

The initiative highlights the capacity to **unite the descendants of Abraham**—Jews, Christians, and Muslims—under a common cause. By focusing on **shared values** such as compassion, healing, and support, **Operation Double Portion** demonstrates the transformative power of **interfaith solidarity**. When faiths come together to champion compassion, healing, and support, they become a powerful force that can bridge even the deepest divides.

Providing Holistic Support

Operation Double Portion delivers **comprehensive care** by addressing:

- **Immediate physical needs** (housing and sustenance).
- **Emotional and psychological well-being**, including **trauma counseling** and **emotional resilience programs**.
- **Community integration**, fostering acceptance and belonging.

Biblical and Theological Foundation: The "Double Portion" Concept

The term **"double portion"** carries profound biblical significance. In **Isaiah 61:7**, the prophet proclaims:
"For your shame ye shall have double; and for confusion they shall rejoice in their portion..."

This verse represents a **divine promise** of **restoration, abundance, and compensation** for loss. For Operation Double Portion, it symbolizes:

- **Restoration of Dignity and Hope**: Offering displaced families a sense of safety and belonging while helping them rebuild their lives.
- **A Legacy of Reconciliation and Peace**: Encouraging families to move beyond past divisions toward a harmonious future.
- **Compensation for Suffering and Loss**: Providing both material restoration and an additional blessing of **compassion, unity, and healing**.

This mission aspires to provide an **"overflowing cup"** of support, embodying **divine compassion**.

Executive Summary: Operation Double Portion in Practice

Operation Double Portion seeks to provide **safe refuge, emotional support, and avenues for peaceful reintegration** for approximately **1,000 families** impacted by the Israeli-Palestinian conflict. This ambitious yet practical initiative emphasizes unity through collaborative host communities, partnerships with local organizations, and extensive cultural programming.

Key Objectives of Operation Double Portion

- **Provide Sanctuary and Stability**: Offer housing and sustenance to families, allowing them to rebuild their lives in a **safe and nurturing environment**.
- **Cultural Integration and Community Engagement**: Facilitate **language classes, cultural orientation,** and **community events** to ensure families feel a genuine sense of belonging in their host communities.
- **Psychological and Emotional Healing**: Implement **trauma counseling** and **emotional resilience programs** to address the profound psychological impacts of displacement.

This initiative is **not just short-term relief** but a **sustainable, forward-looking project** fostering **lasting interfaith unity** and a **new culture of peace**.

Methodology and Approach

Strategic Partnerships with Local Organizations

Operation Double Portion will collaborate with **Palestinian and Israeli organizations** already engaged with affected communities. These partnerships ensure that aid reaches those most in need while respecting cultural sensitivities and unique family needs.

Cultural Integration and Community Engagement

The initiative will focus on fostering a sense of **belonging** by offering:

- **Language classes and cultural orientation programs.**
- **Community events** to promote meaningful exchanges between host communities and refugee families.

These efforts will lead to **greater mutual understanding** and support.

Advocacy, Sustainability, and Global Expansion

A significant component of the project is **advocacy**, aimed at raising awareness about the human impact of the Israeli-Palestinian conflict and encouraging **similar**

initiatives globally. By promoting **peace and sustainability**, the project aspires to inspire a **global movement** rooted in empathy and compassion.

Pilot Project Location: Mahabalipuram, Tamil Nadu

The pilot project will be launched in **Mahabalipuram**, Tamil Nadu, under the auspices of the **Roman Catholic Archdiocese of Chingleput. Most Reverend Antony Sami**, the local Archbishop, has graciously offered accommodations within the Archdiocese's facilities. These will be renovated to create a **welcoming and secure environment** for transitioning families.

Mahabalipuram, a culturally rich and historically significant town, offers an ideal setting for this pilot phase, embodying **diversity, peace,** and **acceptance**. This initial project aims to set a **precedent for similar initiatives worldwide**.

Role of the Roman Catholic Church and Interfaith Support

The **Roman Catholic Church's** involvement exemplifies the **interfaith spirit** of Operation Double Portion. Through **logistical support, outreach,** and **faith-driven compassion**, the Church demonstrates how diverse faith communities can unite toward a common goal.

The project will also engage with **Jewish, Muslim,** and other interfaith organizations globally to create a **network of support and understanding**.

Financial Considerations, Community Involvement, and Long-Term Vision

Financial Transparency and Contributions

Operation Double Portion will rely on funding from **individuals, NGOs, communities,** and **government grants**. Transparency will be paramount, with resources allocated to:

- **Accommodations**
- **Mental health services**
- **Educational programs**
- **Community engagement initiatives**

A **detailed budget** will be prepared and shared with stakeholders to maintain accountability.

Engagement with Local Communities

Local communities will play an active role through **volunteering** and contributing **time and resources**, fostering a **spirit of shared responsibility** and unity.

Long-Term Vision and Expansion

While the pilot phase focuses on Mahabalipuram, **Operation Double Portion** envisions a future where similar programs are established globally. The long-term goal is to create a **ripple effect**, inspiring countries and communities worldwide to adopt this **compassionate model of refugee support**.

A Broader Vision of Peace, Unity, and Responsibility

Operation Double Portion embodies a **vision of society transcending religious, political,** and **cultural divides**. By addressing the **root causes of division** and fostering **interfaith solidarity**, it offers a new paradigm for **peace-building** and **social responsibility**.

As Yaseva, the convenor of the Yeshuan movement, poignantly remarked: **"True compassion sees beyond borders, beyond divisions. It brings us together in our shared humanity."**

Operation Double Portion seeks to embody this vision, representing the spirit of **peace, reconciliation,** and **global unity**.

Conclusion: Building a Legacy of Hope and Restoration

Operation Double Portion stands as a **beacon of hope** in a world often divided by conflict. It provides:

- **Sanctuary for families in need**.
- A model for **interfaith unity**.
- Encouragement for **responsible investment and community engagement**.

Rooted in the biblical notion of a **"double portion,"** this initiative symbolizes **restoration, reconciliation,** and the **abundance** that flows from **compassionate action**.

Through the generosity and collaboration of individuals, communities, and organizations, **Operation Double Portion** aspires to become a **movement**—one that transcends **national, religious,** and **cultural barriers**, embodying a shared commitment to **peace, love,** and **understanding**.

This initiative envisions a world not as it is, but as it **could be**: a world where **empathy overcomes hostility, unity conquers division**, and **compassion leads to enduring peace**.

Operation Double Portion invites all people, all faiths, and all nations to join in building a legacy of healing, joy, and restoration for our shared humanity.

A Call to Action

Operation Double Portion is more than a humanitarian mission—it is a **beacon of hope**. By championing **compassion, interfaith unity, and sustainable support**, it serves as a model for addressing the profound challenges faced by **conflict-torn communities**. This initiative invites descendants of Abraham, along with global supporters, to unite in **faith, love, and action** to restore dignity and rebuild lives.

CHAPTER 24

Conversation Between Yaseva and Dr. Peter Ignatius

Scene: A serene setting at Lake View Life Center, where Yaseva, a visionary championing the cause of Operation Double Portion, meets Dr. Peter Ignatius, the empathetic founder of the center. Known for his deep spirituality and unwavering dedication to humanity, Dr. Ignatius has spent a lifetime committed to serving others. The two sit down to discuss this ambitious initiative, aimed at providing sanctuary and healing for Israeli and Palestinian families torn by conflict.

The Dialogue

Yaseva: Dr. Ignatius, thank you for making time to meet our team today. It's a privilege to sit with someone whose life is such a testament to compassion and purpose. I hope you had the time to review **Operation Double Portion**, an initiative that brings together **descendants of Abraham under a banner of compassion**. We aim to extend a helping hand to those most affected by the conflict between **Israel and Palestine**—families who have lost so much. The goal is to provide them a haven in supportive communities across the globe, including here in **India**, where they can experience **peace, safety, and acceptance**.

Dr. Ignatius: Yaseva, I'm moved by the vision you've laid out. And I can see the potential for profound healing. But, if I'm honest, I have my doubts. These wounds run so deep, with generations having suffered. Do you truly believe that providing refuge and support to a few families can make a significant difference in the larger context?

Yaseva: I understand your skepticism, Dr. Ignatius. The weight of history is indeed heavy. But we're not trying to **erase the past or rewrite it**. Instead, we want to **create a new chapter**, where the focus is on **shared humanity, not lingering resentments**. The past is unchangeable, like clinging to a shadow—it doesn't lead us forward. If we're to hope for a more equitable future, we need to turn our attention toward **building spaces of peace and understanding**. **"Operation Double Portion"** isn't about forgetting, but about **transforming suffering into something life-affirming**.

Dr. Ignatius: That's an inspiring perspective, Yaseva. **Focusing on the future while leaving the bitterness behind** is a powerful approach. Yet, I'm concerned about the present sentiments, particularly in the **U.S.**, where **campus protests and strong anti-Israel sentiments** are intensifying. The students seem disillusioned, perhaps even angry. Do you think **Operation Double Portion** can resonate in this environment?

Yaseva: You're right, Dr. Ignatius. The sentiments are strong, especially among the youth, who are driven by a sense of **justice**. But this isn't simply a political stance. Today's generation is aware of the struggles endured on both sides, especially with the **Palestinian experience of displacement**. There's a powerful empathy that transcends national borders. Many young people today view the **creation of Israel and the displacement of Palestinians** as part of a **colonial legacy**. They see echoes of the past, like the **partition of India and Pakistan in 1947**, which left millions uprooted, scarred, and grieving. These students are speaking up, not out of hatred, but out of a **commitment to justice and human rights**.

Dr. Ignatius: That's true. The memory of the **India-Pakistan partition** is indeed painful, even for those who weren't directly affected. It's understandable that these young voices want to stand for justice, especially when they feel they have the full picture. And today's youth have access to unfiltered stories—**social media, real-time accounts**—they're much more informed about the hardships that Palestinians endure. But I wonder, can this **compassion be channeled positively**?

Yaseva: Exactly, Dr. Ignatius. Today's youth have access to **information that wasn't available before**. They see through narratives that focus only on one side. They're aware of the **trauma and loss on both sides**. This isn't about picking sides but **standing up for those who've suffered**, advocating for the **dignity of every human life**. This is where **Operation Double Portion** offers a transformative solution. Imagine if these **affluent communities** in the U.S., the U.K., and even here in **India** were to open their doors to provide a **safe space for the affected families**. It would not only provide **healing to those directly affected** but would also show the students that action is possible—**real, compassionate action**.

Dr. Ignatius: I can see how that could resonate. **Young people are disillusioned with inaction**. If they could see something tangible—something that brings healing and hope—they might find a new way to channel their energy. A project like **Operation Double Portion** could bridge that gap, giving them a path to work toward peace. But it's more than just providing refuge, isn't it?

Yaseva: Yes, Dr. Ignatius. At its core, **Operation Double Portion** is about **restoring dignity and offering a path to healing**. When **affluent nations** open their doors to these families, it sends a message that the world is ready to **help them rebuild their lives with love, empathy, and respect**. And this approach can resonate deeply on campuses, especially with **students who seek justice** but are uncertain how to achieve it. They don't want to just watch the suffering—they want to **be part of the solution**. By supporting these families, they can find an outlet for their **empathy and their call for justice**.

Dr. Ignatius: I can see how this could bring true healing, not only to those directly impacted but also to the young people advocating for change. When people see **compassion in action**, it reminds them of the good that humanity is capable of. So many students here have **immigrant backgrounds themselves**, and they relate to the struggle of displaced people. It's about **standing with those who are suffering, in solidarity**.

Yaseva: Yes, precisely. Today's students are driven by a **broader vision of justice**, one that isn't confined to geographic or religious boundaries. **Operation Double Portion** allows them to see that **justice doesn't require taking sides** but supporting healing for all. This initiative is a testament to the possibility of uniting **descendants of Abraham** under a shared banner of **empathy and compassion**. It's about choosing **connection over division**, and it gives them a **model to stand for peace and healing** in ways that go beyond protest.

Dr. Ignatius: I can see that this initiative holds **potential to resonate far beyond its immediate goals**. And it's timely, too. Even the **newly elected administration in the U.S.** seems to be aware that student unrest is about more than anger—it's a **call for justice** that can't simply be quieted by policies or police action. **Engaging students and youth leaders** in a constructive effort could change the conversation.

Yaseva: Exactly, Dr. Ignatius. You can't quell the voices of young people who are passionate about **justice with force**. The student body is incredibly **intelligent and informed**. They're speaking out for **human rights, for dignity**. And they see the **injustice in the plight of Palestinians** and the suffering on both sides of this conflict. **Operation Double Portion** provides a **real-world platform to address this human need**, not through words alone but through **action**. It lets students see that there's a **proactive way to contribute** to a legacy of peace.

Dr. Ignatius: I see the power in that. These young people have always sought ways to be involved, to witness **compassion enacted**. If they saw a movement toward healing, something that prioritizes humanity, I believe it would bring a **cathartic shift**—not just for the displaced families but for the students themselves.

Yaseva: Precisely, Dr. Ignatius. This is a movement that has the potential to heal across generations. And that's what **"Operation Double Portion"** stands for—a compassionate, tangible response to centuries of conflict. When communities come together to support these families, it creates a ripple effect. **It transforms suffering into solidarity, trauma into hope, and division into unity.**

Dr. Ignatius: I'm convinced. This initiative is more than a mission; it's a necessary step forward. Let me reach out to my team immediately. We can connect with key leaders in universities and student affairs offices, especially those who are interested in human rights initiatives. I'll also coordinate with local leaders here in India to involve them in securing accommodations. Together, we can provide a safe, welcoming place where families can heal.

Yaseva: That's wonderful, Dr. Ignatius. The **Archbishop of Chingleput** has already expressed his support and is ready to host some of these families in his facilities here. It's crucial that they feel welcome, respected, and given a sense of dignity. **By bringing together these families, we create a community where they aren't just surviving—they're living with a sense of peace and acceptance.** And with allies like you and the Archbishop, we can show the world the true power of compassion.

Dr. Ignatius: This has the potential to leave a lasting legacy. If we offer these families **a life of dignity, respect, and kindness,** we're giving them more than shelter—we're giving them **a new beginning.** This will echo across generations and inspire others to lead with empathy. What you've presented here, Yaseva, is the essence of what it means to live in harmony.

Yaseva: Yes, Dr. Ignatius, that's the heart of **Operation Double Portion.** It's about lifting these families up and helping them build a life where they feel valued and connected. And it's about creating a world where young people see that **peace isn't a distant ideal—it's achievable, here and now, when we choose to stand together.**

Dr. Ignatius: I'm honored to be part of this, Yaseva. **Operation Double Portion** could be a catalyst for peace, **a living testimony of what humanity can accomplish when we step beyond our own borders.** Together, let's bring this vision to life and inspire others to believe in a world built on compassion, justice, and unity.

CHAPTER 25

A Vision of Double Portions and Uniting Destinies

The late evening cast a golden glow over the streets as **Yaseva** and his three-member team exited the office of **Dr. Peter Ignatius**. The air buzzed with excitement—the kind that comes from knowing they had just made a breakthrough. The meeting had been more than productive; it had confirmed their vision for the **Double Portion Project**, a concept born out of the desire to bridge divides and offer hope in a fractured world.

Dr. Ignatius's interest was not just polite; it was enthusiastic—a recognition of the project's potential to make a global impact. For **Yaseva and his team**, this was no small victory. The idea of using their combined experience, faith, and innovation to address the world's most pressing challenges had seemed audacious at first. Now, with support from a respected figure like **Dr. Ignatius**, that audacity felt justified.

The team piled into their vehicle, the hum of the engine underscoring the lively energy inside. **Jerry**, a dynamic team member known for his athleticism and pastoral insight, leaned back in his seat.

"Well, that went better than expected," he said, a broad smile lighting up his face.

"We had a good discussion, didn't we?" Yaseva asked, his tone both reflective and optimistic.

"Absolutely," Jerry replied. **"Dr. Ignatius really got it. He understands how crucial this initiative is."**

The team had discussed many aspects of the **Double Portion Project** with Dr. Ignatius, from its origins to its potential impact. Designed to rehabilitate children traumatized by the conflict in **Palestine** and **Israel**, the project aimed to provide not just shelter but healing. It envisioned creating spaces where trauma could be addressed holistically, using education, community, and joy as tools for recovery.

As the car rolled down the **East Coast Road (ECR)**, past the shimmering coastline and sprawling urban landscapes, **Yaseva** was already thinking ahead.

"You know," he began, breaking a brief silence, **"I think we should extend this Double Portion initiative to the homeless people in the United States."**

Jerry turned toward him, his expression curious. **"Why the USA now?"**

Yaseva's gaze was steady, his tone thoughtful. **"The USA is at a crossroads,"** he said. **"With the recent change in leadership, we're entering a period of transformation. It's the perfect time to act. Our earlier initiatives, like the 'New USA' concept, laid the groundwork for this. And don't forget, the Descendants of Abraham project reinforces the vision of a renewed and united America. The U.S. has always been a symbol of opportunity, but it's time to redefine what that opportunity means—for everyone, including the homeless."**

Jerry nodded slowly, his initial skepticism giving way to understanding. **"That makes sense. So, Double Portion One focuses on the children affected by conflict, and Double Portion Two would address homelessness in America."**

"Exactly," said **Yaseva**. **"The homeless in the U.S. face immense challenges—economic, social, and emotional. A program like Joy Circles could give them not just a place to stay but a sense of purpose and community. We could help rebuild lives from the inside out."**

Dr. Miller, a seasoned strategist whose calm demeanor often grounded the team's discussions, spoke up. **"This dual initiative is groundbreaking. It addresses needs on two different fronts but with the same core values—restoration, dignity, and hope. That's powerful."**

The conversation shifted gears as **Patrick**, the team's resident analyst, brought up a timely topic. **"What do you make of RFK Jr.'s 'Make America Healthy Again (MAHA)' slogan and Trump's 'Make America Great Again (MAGA)'? Both seem to reflect aspirations, but they're very different in tone."**

Miller nodded. **"It's fascinating how slogans like these capture the zeitgeist. But they often lack depth. They don't address the spiritual or emotional dimensions of what greatness or health truly means."**

Yaseva smiled, his eyes lighting up with an idea. **"If I were to revise MAGA,"** he said, **"I'd suggest MAGG: Make America Godly and Great. That's a vision worth pursuing—one that combines morality with resilience."**

Jerry laughed. "That's brilliant! And for MAHA, how about Make America Happy and Healthy All Around? You can't have true greatness without happiness and health." The car erupted in laughter and applause, the team energized by the creativity of their exchange.

As they approached **Anna Nagar**, the tantalizing aroma of nearby eateries reminded them they hadn't eaten since lunch. **"Let's stop here,"** Patrick suggested, pointing to a newly opened Mediterranean restaurant.

The restaurant, with its cozy ambiance and warm lighting, became the backdrop for an even deeper conversation. Over plates of **falafel**, **shawarma**, and **baklava**, the team delved into the essence of what makes a nation truly great.

"Greatness isn't about military might or economic dominance," Patrick said, dipping pita bread into hummus. **"It's about fostering justice, compassion, and peace—values that uplift everyone, not just a select few."**

Miller agreed, his voice thoughtful. **"To be godly, a nation must stop warmongering and start genuinely helping people. America has the resources and influence to lead by example. It's time to use those gifts for good."**

The discussion flowed like a river, meandering through topics of politics, culture, and morality. By the end of the meal, the team felt a renewed sense of purpose. They weren't just talking about solutions; they were laying the groundwork for action.

Back in the car, the conversation took another turn when they tuned into a news channel. **President Donald Trump** was addressing the nation, outlining his plans to curb immigration from Islamic-majority countries. His rhetoric was stark, warning of the dangers posed by **"jihadist threats"** and citing unrest in Europe as a cautionary tale.

Jerry mentioned hearing similar rhetoric from a **Dutch politician**, who had warned about the cultural impact of immigration. **"It's troubling how fear becomes a tool for division,"** he said.

Yaseva, ever reflective, said, "This is why the Descendants of Abraham project is so crucial. We need to counter fear with understanding, division with unity. Just as the stars in the sky shine together without clashing, the

descendants of Abraham can find harmony and purpose."

The metaphor resonated deeply, casting a poetic glow over the team's vision. The stars became a symbol not just of unity but of shared destiny, a reminder that greatness is found in collaboration, not conflict.

When they finally arrived at their office, the night was still young, but their minds were full of ideas. As they stepped out of the vehicle, **Yaseva's phone buzzed**. It was **John Romeo**, his trusted lieutenant. Excusing himself, he took the call, his voice blending with the hum of the city.

Inside, the team began to outline their next steps, the conversations of the day fueling their resolve. They knew the path ahead would be challenging, but they also knew they were on the brink of something extraordinary—a movement that could transform lives, bridge divides, and light up the sky with the brilliance of shared purpose.

CHAPTER 26

Angelic Watchers and the Legacy of St. George

In the divine expanse where the heavens stretch into infinity, **two angels, Jegudiel and Barakiel**, stood as watchful guardians. Ever since their divine connection with **The Yeshuans**, these celestial beings, accompanied by their bands of angels, had committed themselves to a sacred task: to oversee and intercede for **Yaseva** and his mission. Their roles were not passive; they were deeply involved in the spiritual battle unfolding over the earth, particularly in the mission's efforts to uplift the descendants of Abraham.

The angels observed with great fascination as the **International Virtual Conclave of the Yeshuans** took shape. This conclave was not just a gathering of human leaders; it was a divine convergence, focusing on the descendants of Abraham, whose legacy had profound significance in God's plan for humanity. For **Jegudiel and Barakiel**, this mission was more than a strategy—it was a sacred unfolding of God's purpose, one that could shape the future of the world.

The angels, in constant intercession before God, prayed earnestly for the conclave's success. They saw the sincerity of the Yeshuan mission, which sought to expand God's reign on Earth—a realm built on **love, peace, and joy**. To the angels, this mission was nothing less than the manifestation of God's will for a fractured and hurting world.

The Double Portion Vision Takes Root

As the mission progressed, a new dimension was introduced through the concept of the **Double Portion Project**, which **Yaseva** had recently discussed with **Dr. Peter Ignatius**. The angels marveled at the vision's audacity and depth. It wasn't just about addressing immediate needs; it was about bringing **abundance where there had been scarcity, joy where there had been despair, and healing where there had been pain**.

When Dr. Peter initially hesitated to fully embrace the project, **Jegudiel and Barakiel** became even more fervent in their intercession. They stood before God, advocating for divine inspiration to touch Dr. Peter's heart.
"Grant him the wisdom to see the beauty of this vision," they pleaded, **"and**

the courage to act in accordance with Your will."

Their prayers did not go unanswered. The **Spirit moved within Dr. Peter**, softening his heart and illuminating his understanding. As he began to see the mission's potential, the angels rejoiced, their praise reverberating through the heavens. They knew this was a pivotal moment, a sign that God's hand was guiding every step of the mission.

Angels Guarding the Path

As **Yaseva** and the Yeshuans team delved deeper into their work, seeking to align the United States with a vision of **godliness and greatness**, the angels took their roles as protectors and guides with renewed vigor. They overshadowed the team with **divine protection**, warding off spiritual attacks and ensuring that the mission remained steadfast in its purpose.

The angels also prayed persistently for the descendants of Abraham, that they might rise above divisions and live out their destiny as God's chosen people. They envisioned a world where these descendants would **shine like stars in the sky**, reflecting God's glory and serving as a beacon of hope for all humanity.

The angels marveled at the **Spirit's inspiration**, which led **Yaseva** and his team to blend **vision with action, spirituality with strategy**. They praised God for orchestrating a mission that not only addressed earthly needs but also pointed people toward eternal truths.

A Heavenly Role Model: St. George

In their reflections, **Jegudiel and Barakiel** turned their thoughts to **St. George**, an early martyr of the Christian faith whose life exemplified **courage, sacrifice, and unwavering devotion to God**. St. George's story had transcended centuries, becoming a symbol of **hope and inspiration** for countless believers.

Born in **Palestine**, St. George's legacy was rooted in his martyrdom under the persecution of **Roman Emperor Diocletian**. But it was his legendary act of **slaying the dragon to rescue a princess** that captured the imagination of the world. For the angels, this tale was more than a legend; it was a powerful metaphor for **Yeshua's redemptive work** in rescuing His bride—the Church—from the clutches of evil.

The **overcoming spirit of St. George** resonated deeply with the Yeshuan mission. It symbolized **triumph over violence, enmity, and conflict**. For **Jegudiel and Barakiel**, St. George embodied the very essence of what the mission sought to achieve: **delivering humanity from the chains of animosity and despair** and leading them toward a life of **joy and peace**.

A Providential Call

As the angels pondered the significance of St. George's legacy, a **phone call** came to **Yaseva** from **John Romeo**, his trusted lieutenant. The call carried unexpected but extraordinary news: a friend in the **United States** wished to sell a property near the **shrine of St. George** in **Edathua**, a coastal town in **Kerala** along India's backwaters.

The shrine of **St. George** was no ordinary place. For centuries, it had drawn pilgrims from around the world, people seeking the saint's **intercession for healing, protection, and guidance**. The shrine stood as a testament to the power of faith and the enduring legacy of St. George's life.

To the angels, this proposal was not merely a coincidence—it was a **divine connection**. They saw it as a sign of **God's providence**, an opportunity to establish a physical base for the mission under the patronage of **St. George**.

Building Under the Banner of St. George

The idea of linking the **Yeshuan mission** with **St. George's legacy** filled **Yaseva** and his team with excitement and inspiration. Establishing a base near the shrine would not only provide a strategic advantage but also imbue the mission with **spiritual significance**.

For **Jegudiel and Barakiel**, this connection was profound. They envisioned the shrine as a place where the descendants of Abraham could come together, **shedding divisions** and **embracing their shared heritage**. They believed that under the banner of **St. George**, the mission could inspire a movement of **reconciliation and unity**, one that would ripple across nations and generations.

Shining Like Stars

With the intercession of the angels and the patronage of **St. George**, the mission began to take on a **celestial quality**. The prophecy of the **descendants of**

Abraham shining like stars in the sky seemed closer than ever. To the angels, this was not just a poetic image; it was a **divine promise**, a vision of humanity living in harmony with God and one another.

The angels imagined a world transformed by the mission's work—a world where **joy replaced sorrow, peace replaced conflict, and love replaced hatred**. They saw the descendants of Abraham not as fragmented groups but as a **unified people**, reflecting God's glory and fulfilling their divine purpose.

A Divine Journey Continues

As **Yaseva** and his team prepared to move forward, they were filled with a sense of **awe and responsibility**. They knew they were part of something far greater than themselves—a movement orchestrated by **God**, guided by **angels**, and inspired by **saints**.

The journey ahead was daunting, but they were undeterred. With **angels as their guardians, St. George as their patron, and God as their guide**, they marched forward, ready to fulfill their destiny. They carried with them the hope that their work would **light up the world**, just as the stars light up the heavens.

This was no ordinary mission. It was a **divine calling**, a sacred task to bring **heaven to earth** and to reveal God's love to a world desperately in need of it. And as they moved forward, they did so with the conviction that **the best was yet to come**.

CHAPTER 27

The Call to Edathua and the Global Vision of Redemption

It began with a simple yet profound phone call. **John Romeo**, one of **Yaseva's closest confidants**, reached out with a message that would alter the course of their mission. His voice carried a mix of urgency and excitement as he shared the news: **a property in Edathua**, nestled along the serene backwaters of Kerala and adjacent to the historic shrine of **St. George**, was being offered to the **Yeshuans**. The owner, a close associate from the United States, had felt inspired to make this property available, seeing it as part of a greater purpose.

To **Yaseva**, this was no coincidence. **It was a divine appointment**, a clear sign of God's providence. Only moments earlier, the angels had been invoking God's mercies and grace over the mission. This offer was more than land; it was **an affirmation from heaven**, a tangible expression of God's hand guiding their steps.

The Spirit of St. George: A Divine Mascot

The shrine of **St. George**, renowned across centuries, became the symbolic heart of the mission. **St. George**, a martyr whose legacy spanned continents—from England to Georgia, Russia, and beyond—was more than a saint. **He was a unifying figure**, a symbol of resilience and triumph over adversity. His story of slaying the dragon and rescuing the princess paralleled the mission's calling to protect the innocent and overcome the forces of darkness in the modern age.

St. George was envisioned as the spiritual patron of the **Redemption Children's Home**, one of the **Yeshuans' most urgent and ambitious initiatives**. This project aimed to address the global tragedy of **abortion**—a persistent darkness that extinguished the lives of thousands of unborn children daily. These innocent souls, robbed of life, became the focus of the **Yeshuans' prayers and efforts**.

The establishment of **Redemption Children's Centers and Homes** was more than a humanitarian effort; **it was a divine mandate**. Guided by the spirit of God and the protection of St. George, these centers would provide **shelter, support, and hope** for mothers and children alike. The message was clear: **God's care begins at conception**, and **every life, no matter how small, carries divine purpose.**

This profound truth became the cornerstone of the Yeshuans' mission, but it didn't stop there. Redemption Children's Centers would be just the beginning. The vision expanded to encompass the creation of **Joy Cities**, with a goal of establishing 2,000 such cities worldwide by 2030. These cities would be beacons of peace, joy, and community, places where humanity could thrive in harmony with God and one another.

Securing the Land for God's Purpose

As **Yaseva** absorbed the magnitude of the opportunity, he felt an overwhelming sense of responsibility. The property in Edathua, with its proximity to the shrine of St. George, was destined to be the foundation for a global movement. Yet, practical challenges loomed. **Finances** would be required to secure the land and begin the work, but **Yaseva was undeterred**. He placed his trust in God, recalling the scripture that declared **God's provision for those who labor in His name**.

"Where God guides, He provides," murmured **Yaseva**, a quiet prayer rising from his heart. This unwavering faith fueled his determination, knowing that the resources would come, for the mission was rooted in **divine purpose**.

The Joy Dome: A Flotilla of Peace

As if divinely timed, another inspiration struck. **Yaseva** recalled the recent discussions at the **international virtual conclave** led by **Commander Abdul Rauf**. The concept of **The Joy Dome**, a flotilla destined to sail across the Mediterranean, had been proposed as a **hub for peace and learning**. Now, it became clear: **St. George would be its spiritual mascot**.

The **Joy Dome** was not just a vessel; **it was a movement**, a living testament to the **power of joy to transform lives**. Onboard, youth from various nations would participate in diploma programs focused on the **art of peace and joy**. These teachings, grounded in wisdom and faith, would empower a new generation to embrace **reconciliation and healing**.

"Blessed are the peacemakers, for they shall be called the sons and daughters of God," Yaseva reflected. The Joy Dome would embody this truth, carrying the message of peace to regions long mired in conflict.

In this mission, St. George's sword took on a new form—not a weapon of war, but a symbol of joy and triumph over despair. The Joy Dome would pierce through the darkness, liberating hearts and inspiring nations to pursue lasting peace.

Defeating the Dragon of Darkness

The imagery of **St. George slaying the dragon** resonated deeply with the mission. The dragon, symbolic of **violence, despair, and division**, was a fitting metaphor for the forces that had long plagued humanity. But this time, **the dragon would be defeated not by physical force but by the overwhelming power of joy, love, and reconciliation**.

The mission saw the **Middle East**, a region scarred by centuries of conflict, as a key focus. The **Joy Dome** would dock in ports across the region, offering **hope and healing** to communities yearning for change. It was a bold vision, but one rooted in the unshakable belief that **joy could overcome even the deepest divisions**.

Mobilizing a Global Network

Elated by the unfolding plan, **Yaseva** immediately shared the news with **Commander Abdul Rauf**. The commander, a visionary in his own right, was thrilled. He suggested reaching out to **ship operators in Russia, Cyprus, and other regions** where St. George was revered. These connections could galvanize support for the initiative, creating a **global network united under the banner of peace and joy**.

The mission's reach was expanding rapidly, and the possibilities seemed limitless. With each step, it became clearer that this was no ordinary undertaking. It was a divine movement, guided by God and supported by a host of earthly and heavenly allies.

Heaven Rejoices

In the celestial realms, the angels celebrated the unfolding plan. **Jegudiel and Barakiel**, who had been interceding tirelessly, lifted their voices in praise. They saw in this mission the **fulfillment of God's promises**, a clear signal of His **mercy and grace**.

The vision of **love, peace, and joy becoming a reality** was breathtaking. The **descendants of Abraham**, long divided, were being drawn together by a **shared purpose**. The angels saw a glimpse of humanity's future—a future where **people of all nations would shine like stars**, reflecting the glory of their Creator.

A Miraculous Path Forward

As **Yaseva** joined the angels in jubilation, he felt a deep sense of **gratitude**. This was not just a mission; **it was a calling**, a path toward humanity's ultimate **redemption and unity**. The challenges ahead were daunting, but the vision was clear, and the **promise of God's faithfulness** gave them strength.

With the **shrine of St. George as their foundation**, the **Redemption Children's Centers, Joy Cities**, and **The Joy Dome** would serve as **beacons of hope** in a dark world. And with the **power of joy as their weapon**, the Yeshuans would continue their journey, **lighting up the sky with the brilliance of God's love**.

The dragon would fall, the stars would shine, and the world would be transformed.

CHAPTER 28

Introducing MAGGA, The Transformation of Nations

The stillness of the pre-dawn hours hung heavy as **Yaseva** sat in the quiet solitude of his study. The weight of the recent conversation with his trusted lieutenant, **John Romeo**, lingered in his mind. The news about the property near the **St. George Shrine in Edathua** was not merely an opportunity—it was **a divine sign**, a confirmation that their mission was in alignment with **heaven's plan.**

The shrine, a place steeped in centuries of devotion and miracles, would serve as **a spiritual anchor** for the **Joy Dome initiative**. This bold and unprecedented project, spearheaded by **Commander Abdul Rauf**, aimed to establish **a flotilla of peace in the Mediterranean**. But it was more than a logistical undertaking; **it was a mission to ignite hearts, heal divisions, and spread joy to port cities across the globe**.

Adding to this profound sense of purpose was the recent dialogue with **Dr. Peter Ignatius** about the **"double portion"** initiative. This concept, rooted in the promise of abundance, symbolized the team's unwavering commitment to **expanding God's reign on Earth**—a reign defined by **love, peace, and joy**.

The Stars of Abraham: A Heavenly Mandate

As the minutes ticked toward dawn, **Yaseva's thoughts** turned to the **descendants of Abraham**, envisioned as **stars shining brightly** in the vast expanse of the heavens. Each star represented **a life of purpose, a legacy of faith**, and a testament to humanity's potential to reflect **divine light**. This imagery was more than poetic; it was **a call to action**.

The descendants of Abraham were scattered across the globe, their diversity spanning faiths, cultures, and nations. Yet, in this diversity lay the potential for **unity**—a unity that could inspire **transformative change**. The vision of these stars compelled **Yaseva** to ask himself a crucial question: **Which path should take precedence?** The opportunities before him were vast, but clarity was imperative.

The Spirit of Unasked Offering

Amid his contemplations, an unexpected thought struck him: **Elon Musk**. News had emerged about Musk's **staggering quarter-billion-dollar contribution** to **President Trump's election campaign**, a gesture made **without expectation or publicity**. Musk's act of **"unasked offering"** was driven by **a shared vision**—peace, health, and the good for America.

This resonated deeply with **Yaseva**, who had long practiced the principle of **'Unasked Offerings.'** For him, the act of giving without expectation was a cornerstone of the mission. **Such selfless generosity held the power to transform**, to bring life and hope where it was least expected. It was a reminder that **greatness lies not in taking, but in giving**.

The Call to Act

By now, it was **4:00 a.m.**, and while his core team rested, **Yaseva** felt an urgency he could not ignore. **Time was slipping away**, and decisions needed to be made. Should he wait until the morning or act now? The weight of the moment demanded action.

By **5:30 a.m.**, he had resolved to convene his team. One by one, he dialed their numbers: **John Romeo, Commander Abdul Rauf, Manjula Dev, Jerry, Patrick the political analyst, and Dr. Vinod Miller**. Though groggy, each team member understood the **gravity of the early call**.

A Vision Unfolds

As their faces appeared on the screen, **Yaseva** greeted them warmly. **"Good morning, my friends. I appreciate you joining so early. We have much to discuss, and your insights are invaluable."**

He paused, his voice steady with purpose. **"You all understand the transformative power of unasked offering—giving life where it was never expected, bringing hope and change in unexpected places. This principle has been the cornerstone of our journey."**

The team nodded, their attentiveness reflecting their trust in his leadership. **"Our mission stands at a crossroads,"** Yaseva stated solemnly. **"In fact, the whole world is at a crossroads."**

The team nodded in agreement.

"God, in all prudence, has placed leaders in the USA who acknowledge His sovereignty, authority, and majesty," Yaseva emphasized. **"Getting the U.S. people and nation 'God Aligned' will surely make America great, like it has never been before—more than what Americans can ask or imagine!"**

He then revealed with passion, **"This is why I decided to pull you out of your sleep! To announce MAGGA—Make America Great and God Aligned!"**

Close to **President Trump's MAGA,** but **way ahead in terms of potentials and possibilities!** The team erupted in joy, **Patrick raising a High-5.**
"Thank you," Yaseva acknowledged graciously, while emphasizing, **"Time is of the essence, and we must act swiftly before the new U.S. administration takes charge in mid-January."**

Integrating MAGGA and MAHHA

Before closing the momentous meeting, **Yaseva expanded on his vision:** **"Through MAGGA, we can integrate our projects—empowering grassroots communities with Joy Circles and addressing global crises through initiatives like Commander Rauf's flotilla. Imagine spreading joy to port cities worldwide, transforming them into centers of peace and prosperity."**

"The descendants of Abraham," he continued, **"will actively participate in this magnificent spectrum of initiatives to make America great and God aligned."**

The call to action resonated deeply, filling the team with **a renewed sense of purpose.** They knew they were not just participants but **leaders in a divine mission**—one that would redefine greatness by aligning it with **God's principles.**

He emphasized the broader scope.

"This aligns with another priority—**MAHHA: Make America Happy and Healthy All Around,** inspired by RFK Jr.'s health initiatives. Together, **MAGGA** and **MAHHA** can make the United States **a model nation** by the descendants of Abraham in the U.S., paving the way for **global transformation.**

Empowering the Descendants of Abraham

As **Yaseva** spoke, his passion intensified.
"**This mission includes empowering the descendants of Abraham, helping them rise to their destiny as stars in the sky. The spectrum of the ninefold descendants—Jews, Muslims, Christians, Saivites, Vaishnavites, Buddhists, Jains, and Yeshuans, including all who pursue joy with love-occupied hearts—are all represented in the United States. This land, where freedom has long flourished, is ready to become both Godly and Great.**"

The Descendants of Abraham in the USA will be **a solid force** alongside **President Trump**, aligning the nation with **the will of God** in multiple ways, **expanding the reign of peace and joy in the land.** They will be given **special inputs and capacity building** to become **Joypreneurs**, specializing in sectors appropriate to their **skills, talents, and strengths, converting challenges into opportunities** and creating initiatives that **benefit the people and the country**.

He paused, letting the gravity of his words settle.
"**Friends, this is our moment to act. Through MAGGA we can transform America into a beacon of light for the world, tackling critical issues such as conflicts and wars, holistic well-being of citizens, unemployment, climate change, empowering grassroots communities, and spreading joy as waters cover the sea. This mission is tremendous, and together, we will fulfill it.**"

A Unified Resolve

As **Yaseva finished**, the screen lit up with reactions—**thumbs-up, claps, and smiles of solidarity.** The team, though tired, felt energized by the shared vision.

"**All praise to Yeshua and the Yeshuans,**" Yaseva said, closing the call. The team dispersed, each carrying a renewed sense of purpose.

As dawn broke over the horizon, **Yaseva gazed out his window,** the light of the rising sun **a reminder of the divine light guiding their mission.** The path ahead was daunting, but the **promise of transformation** gave them strength. Together, they would fulfill the vision of **MAGGA** and **MAHHA**, bringing **joy, healing, and hope** to a world in desperate need.

SECTION G - "THE CALL OF DESTINY FOR THE DESCENDANTS OF ABRAHAM"

The Rise of the Joyist Unasked Offering Movement

The quiet hours before dawn had often been a time of profound clarity for **Yaseva**, but on this particular morning, his thoughts carried an extraordinary weight. The recent discussions with his lieutenants and team had revolved around a concept that was swiftly becoming the cornerstone of their mission: **the Joyist Unasked Offering Movement.**

This idea, rooted in **selfless giving and proactive generosity**, resonated deeply with everyone involved. It was no longer about waiting to be called upon but stepping forward willingly, offering one's **skills, resources, and talents** to further the divine mission of gathering the descendants of Abraham under the banners of **peace, harmony, and joy.**

Manjula Dev's Call to Action

The first response came from **Manjula Dev**, the articulate and passionate spokesperson for the **Yeshuans Redemption Children's Mission**. Her voice brimmed with excitement as she congratulated **Yaseva** on the bold step forward.

"Wonderful, Yaseva," she began. **"This Unasked Offering Movement is truly inspiring. As my contribution, I've decided to involve my niece, Santina, and form a team to meet the Bishop of Chengalpattu. We'll present the vision of Saint George's Redemption Children's Home and the War-Traumatized Children's Home, requesting temporary use of the diocese's unused buildings for this noble cause."**

"What do you think?" she asked eagerly.
"That's wonderful,"Yaseva replied, his enthusiasm evident. **"Let's move this forward quickly."**

Manjula assured him,"I'll take care of it. We'll meet the bishop soon and set the wheels in motion."

But her ideas didn't stop there. **"Since I speak Malayalam,"** she added, **"I could connect with the leaders in Edathua, where John Romeo mentioned the training center for the Double Portion Mission. This center could train** individuals to support these projects. I'll establish an ecumenical partnership, gathering missionaries and equipping women with skills in midwifery, counseling, and leadership."

Her vision was grand: a **network of trained individuals** dedicated to bringing **love, peace, and joy** to communities worldwide. As the call ended, both felt the spark of **divine alignment** propelling them forward.

A Call from Commander Abdul Rauf

As soon as the conversation with **Manjula** ended, **Yaseva** noticed his phone buzzing. It was **Commander Abdul Rauf**, the man tasked with leading the ambitious **flotilla project**. Intrigued, **Yaseva** quickly returned the call.

"Good morning, Commander," he greeted warmly.
"Good morning, Yaseva," Rauf replied, his voice charged with energy. **"I've been reflecting on your talk about the Joyist Unasked Offering Movement. It's a truly transformative idea. The potential it holds is immense. Most people hesitate to act because the world is so focused on immediate returns. But this movement—offering without expectation—cuts through that mindset. It's profoundly divine."**

"Since joining your team, I've realized the power of this concept," Rauf continued. **"Under the banner of the Unasked Offering, individuals can contribute their talents and skills freely. This isn't just inspirational; it's revolutionary."**

Rauf's thoughts turned to the flotilla project, a visionary initiative to **spread joy and peace across the Mediterranean.**
"Imagine a fleet of vessels promoting harmony among nations and cultures," he said. **"This flotilla could pave the way for global unity and cultural exchange. And to that end, I've identified some ships that might fit our needs."**

"Tell me more," said **Yaseva**, intrigued.
"There's a ship that can accommodate 300 passengers," Rauf explained. **"It's about 120 meters long, with a draft of 5.5 meters and a beam of 22 meters. I believe it's perfect for our mission."**

"That sounds promising," replied **Yaseva** with a chuckle. "Though I must admit, you've delved into the technical details a bit more than I expected!"

Commander Rauf laughed."I wanted to ensure we have the best options. I'm also drafting a proposal titled 'Empowering Global Harmony,' which could help attract partnerships and funding for the Joyist Flotilla. What do you think?"
"That's an excellent idea," said Yaseva. "We need to take concrete steps to make this vision a reality. Hiring ships seems more practical than purchasing them outright."

"Exactly," Rauf agreed. "And there's another initiative we discussed—the Diploma at Sea program. I think it's a brilliant concept. Imagine students from around the world coming aboard to learn about promoting peace and joy. We could offer immersive week-long programs, followed by extended stays at port cities for community projects."

"That's fantastic," said Yaseva."This program could shape a new generation of leaders committed to harmony and joy."

The Tech Vision of Imran Namazi

Later in the day, **Imran Namazi,** the tech-savvy strategist, reached out to share his thoughts.
"Hi, Yaseva," he began. "This Unasked Offering Movement is brilliant. It's proactive, joy-oriented, and exactly what the world needs right now. The term 'Joyist Unasked Offering' is perfect. It embodies everything this initiative stands for."

The Rise of the Joyist Unasked Offering Movement

Imran laughed as he added, "The world has been plagued by so many negative narratives. This movement can be the tipping point, not just for our initiative but for global transformation. It can create a more equitable and inclusive society."

"I completely agree," said Yaseva. "Surely, these are words of wisdom."

"I also have some good news," Imran continued. "I've identified a group that specializes in virtual conferences. Let's organize a Global MAGGA

Exhibition online. It's the perfect way to showcase this movement to the world. I've already contacted a friend in the U.S. who can help connect us with influential networks."

"That's an excellent idea," said Yaseva. "A virtual conference could amplify our message far beyond what we imagined."

The Angels Rejoice

Meanwhile, in the heavenly realms, **the angels watched with joy and anticipation.** They marvelled at the beauty of the **Joyist Unasked Offering Movement**, understanding its divine significance.

"This is a game-changer," they declared, their voices filled with praise. **"These actions, born from selflessness and love, will steer humanity away from destruction and toward God's light."**

The angels interceded with God, praying for His grace to inspire more people to embrace this movement. They envisioned a world where individuals offered their skills and strengths freely, not out of obligation but as fragrant offerings to God.

The Countdown to MAGGA: A Vision for the Ages

The discussions about the **Joyist Unasked Offering Movement** had set the tone for a transformative journey. For days, **Yaseva** and his team had explored ideas and possibilities that resonated with the divine calling to unite the descendants of Abraham and ignite the vision of **MAGGA—Make America Great and God-Aligned.** Yet, as the hours slipped by, an undeniable tension lingered.

The challenge was immense. **The clock was ticking toward January 20, 2025,** the date when the new U.S. government would take office. For MAGGA to be unveiled with the impact it deserved, the team had to act swiftly and decisively. **Yaseva** understood the stakes: this was not just about unveiling a vision but about ensuring it was **God-centred, uplifting, and inclusive—a tapestry that wove together the efforts of the descendants of Abraham with a singular purpose: glorifying God and transforming lives.**

As evening descended, the dark monsoon clouds rolled over the horizon, casting the sea into a deep, inky blue. The landscape mirrored **Yaseva's inner conflict,** yet amidst the gathering gloom, a dramatic shaft of light broke through the clouds in the west. It illuminated a patch of water, a striking reminder of hope in the midst of darkness.

The symbolism was not lost on him. **Yaseva realized that time, his fiercest competitor, was slipping away.** He could not afford indecision. The vision of MAGGA demanded **urgency, clarity, and action.** With a heart filled with resolve, he made a decision.

"Yes, we will go this way," he affirmed aloud, as if declaring it to the heavens. Picking up his phone, he dialed a trusted collaborator—his architect friend, **Bhavana**, who had worked with him on a number of visionary projects in the past.

A Virtual Vision Takes Shape

Explaining the vision of **MAGGA** to Bhavana, **Yaseva** outlined his plan for a virtual exhibition—a digital walk-through experience that would transcend physical boundaries and reach a global audience. The traditional approach of organizing a physical exhibition in the U.S. was impractical given the tight timeline. In the digital age, a virtual expo was not just a necessity but an opportunity to amplify their message to an international audience.

Bhavana listened intently, her creative mind already mapping out possibilities. **"It's an ambitious plan,"** she admitted, **"but it can be done. We'll need to mobilize a large team quickly and work around the clock. Are you ready for that kind of commitment?"**

"We have no choice," replied Yaseva firmly. **"This is our moment to act. We must show the world the power of God-aligned leadership and the potential of uniting the descendants of Abraham."**

What followed were weeks of relentless effort. Emails flew back and forth, virtual meetings stretched into the early hours, and brainstorming sessions sparked a flood of ideas. The team, **fueled by faith and a shared sense of purpose**, worked tirelessly to bring the vision to life.

Bhavana assembled a talented group of designers, developers, and technologists. Together, they crafted an **immersive experience** that would not only inform but inspire. The virtual exhibition was envisioned as a transformative journey, showcasing the potential of **MAGGA** to create a harmonious, God-aligned America.

The exhibit would feature **interactive displays, testimonies, and stories of hope.** It would highlight the contributions of the descendants of Abraham—the **Stars in the Sky**—and their shared legacy of faith and resilience. It would celebrate **innovation, peace, and the power of unasked offerings** to transform communities and nations.

The Grand Unveiling: A Monumental Moment

Finally, the day arrived. The team gathered with eager anticipation to witness the first preview of the initiative they had poured their hearts into:

"MAGGA: Make America Great and God-Aligned – The Joy of All Americans"
An entrepreneurial and transformative expo, presented by the **Yeshuans**—the descendants of Abraham, the **"Stars in the Sky."**
Supported by **GEN (Global Ecumenical Network)** and the **Joyist International Movement.**

The **virtual exhibition** was nothing short of breathtaking. As the preview unfolded, it became clear that this was more than a group of innovative projects; it was a **manifestation of transformation of the highest degree.**

A Showcase of Unity and Innovation

The exhibition opened with a compelling introduction to the vision of **MAGGA.** Through immersive visuals and stirring narratives, it depicted a harmonious future where America embraced its destiny as a God-aligned nation. Each section of the exhibit focused on a different pillar of the movement:

- **Faith as a Foundation:** Showcasing the role of spiritual alignment in guiding America toward its divine purpose.
- **Unity Across Communities:** Highlighting the contributions of the ninefold descendants of Abraham.
- **Joyist Initiatives:** Presenting actionable projects like Joy Circles, Double Portion Homes, and the Joy Dome flotilla.
- **Sustainable Progress:** Addressing critical global challenges such as climate change, health inequities, and unemployment.

Interactive features allowed viewers to engage directly with the content, leaving comments, making pledges, and even signing up to volunteer or support the initiatives.

As the team watched the preview, they were overwhelmed with emotion. The exhibition was more than a showcase of ideas; it was a **testament to the power of faith, unity, and creativity.** It stood as a bold declaration that a **God-aligned America** could be a **beacon of hope for the world.**

For **Yaseva,** it was a moment of profound gratitude. He knew this was not the end but the **beginning of something extraordinary.** The virtual exhibition was a platform that could **inspire nations, uplift countless lives,** and glorify God in ways they had only dreamed of.

A Global Call to Action

The unveiling of the virtual exhibition marked the **start of a global call to action.** Supported by the **Global Ecumenical Network (GEN)** and the **Joyist International Movement,** the initiative began to gather momentum. The support of leaders from across the world was solicited, and individuals from various walks of life were inspired to join the movement.

The **descendants of Abraham, symbolized as stars in the sky,** shone brightly in this new chapter of human history. Through their collective efforts, they were not just transforming America—they were **creating a ripple effect that would impact the world.**

A Beacon of Light in the Darkness

As the evening gave way to night, the dramatic shaft of light that had pierced the monsoon clouds earlier seemed to linger in **Yaseva's mind.** It was a reminder that even in the darkest moments, **hope could shine through.**

The **virtual exhibition** was that light—a **beacon of hope, joy, and transformation** that could guide humanity toward a **brighter, God-aligned future.**

With **faith as their foundation** and **unity as their strength,** the Yeshuans pressed forward, determined to make MAGGA a reality and to glorify God in all they did.

The Joyist Movement in Action

As the day progressed, **Yaseva** reflected on the flurry of activity and the incredible energy surrounding the **Joyist Unasked Offering Movement.** Each conversation—whether with **Manjula, Commander Rauf,** or **Imran**—revealed **new facets of the mission,** weaving together a tapestry of extraordinary **hope, joy, and divine purpose.**

This movement was more than an initiative—it was the **beginning of a new chapter in human history.** A chapter marked by **selfless giving, unity,** and the pursuit of a **God-aligned destiny.** The **descendants of Abraham, envisioned as stars shining brightly in the heavens,** were now coming together, their **collective light illuminating the path toward a brighter, more harmonious world.**

In line with the vision of the **present leadership of the U.S.,** which sought to move away from wars, weapon-based economies, compromised health systems, and other such negativity, MAGGA offered an inspired way forward.

The Launch of MAGGA: A Divine Timing

With unwavering faith and a clear vision, **Yaseva** and his team pressed forward, knowing they were part of something far greater than anything existing in the world. Together, they would **transform lives, inspire nations,** and **glorify God** through their work.

The date for the **Launch of MAGGA** was fixed for **January 6, 2025**—the **Feast of the Three Kings from the East,** who came following the **Star of Bethlehem** to worship the babe **Yeshua.** MAGGA was certainly a **'Gift from the East,'** brought by **Kings of Peace and Joy,** with **the Stars in the Skies bearing witness.**

Heaven and Earth in Harmony

The angels sang in celebration, their voices echoing through the heavens. And on earth, the **Joyist Unasked Offering Movement** began to take root, spreading its **message of hope and joy** to every corner of the globe.

As the stars illuminated the night sky, they symbolized the mission's promise: a world transformed by faith, unity, and love, shining with the glory of God and the collective light of His people.

CHAPTER 30

The Unveiling of MAGGA: A Vision for a New Era

As the **6ᵗʰ of January 2025** drew near, excitement gripped everyone involved. The decision to launch **MAGGA—Make America Great and God-Aligned—on the Feast of the Magi** was deeply symbolic. It was a declaration of **hope and transformation** for the year ahead. This massive **entrepreneurial and transformative initiative,** led by the **Yeshuans and the Descendants of Abraham,** sought to inspire a **God-aligned future for America and the world.**

The venue was a spectacle of activity. The setting was festive, with large cut-outs of **MAGGA** strategically placed. A massive screen, which would display the **MAGGA Virtual Expo,** dominated the centre stage.

MAGGA Team members were dressed in **colourful coats boldly displaying the letters MAGGA** on their backs. These **'Coats of Many Colours'** symbolized **multiple blessings from God Almighty.** The atmosphere was electric with **excitement and expectancy.**

Word of the launch had reached high places. Invitations had been sent to **The President,** key members of the incoming U.S. administration, including **RFK Jr.,** the Health Secretary, and leaders from departments of **education, labor, and other sectors** pivotal to the vision of making America truly great.

The Moment Arrives

As the clock ticked closer to midnight, the room was alive with chatter and anticipation. **Dinner had been served,** and the conversations buzzed with discussions about the potential impact of MAGGA. This wasn't just an initiative—it was a **movement poised to redefine leadership** in alignment with **God's principles.**

At last, **Yaseva** took to the stage. His demeanor was calm yet commanding, his presence immediately captivating. As the audience subsided into silence, the room dimmed, and he began to speak.

"Thank you, my friends," he started, his voice carrying the weight of the moment. **"It's an honor to stand here on the cusp of a new year, a**

new chapter, and, I hope, a new era for our world. Tonight, we launch MAGGA—not just as a vision, but as a call to action. A call to align ourselves with what is noble, admirable, excellent, and praiseworthy. Let us embrace this journey with faith, hope, and love."

After his brief address, he added, **"What you are about to see is a testament to the collective effort of everyone involved."**

MAGGA: The Virtual Experience

The room fell silent as the screen lit up, accompanied by **pulsating background music** that perfectly matched the grandeur of the occasion. The title **MAGGA: Make America Great and God-Aligned** appeared on the screen, framed by **red stripes symbolizing the unity and strength of the USA.**

The screen transitioned into the first pavilion of the virtual exposition. **'Joy of All Americans'** flashed across the screen, accompanied by the vibrant face of a guide, who greeted the audience with a **beaming smile.**

Welcome to the Six Mega Pavilions of the MAGGA Exposition

The screen illuminated with the title, **"Welcome to the Six Mega Pavilions,"** and the room buzzed with anticipation. The guide, her voice brimming with excitement, announced:
"These six pavilions showcase a breathtaking spectrum of 21 Exhibit Panels—a symphony of special skills, revolutionary strategies, and visionary systems. Together, they unveil the roadmap to Make America Great and God-Aligned with unmatched precision and rapidity!"

She gestured toward the panels, adding, **"Each exhibit features QR Codes that unlock a treasure trove of deeper insights and interactive content. Immerse yourself in this transformative journey."**

With a dazzling flourish, the visual zoomed into the **first pavilion,** setting the stage for an **awe-inspiring adventure.**

PAVILION 1

Exhibit Panel 1: HALOH - A Love-Occupied Heart – Unlock the Ideal Human Operating System

Embrace **love as the core principle of your life** and unlock optimized performance, inner fulfillment, harmonious relationships, resilience, and personal growth. **Reboot your heart, upgrade your connections, and optimize your life** for joy, purpose, and boundless potential.

Main Concept:

Transform your life by making **love the core principle of your operating system**, unlocking optimized performance, inner fulfillment, and harmonious relationships.

Key Benefits:

1. **Optimized Performance:**

   - Love fuels creativity, passion, and motivation, enhancing productivity and achievements.

2. **Inner Fulfillment:**

   - A heart centered on love brings purpose, contentment, and lasting joy.

3. **Harmonious Relationships:**

   - Empathy and compassion deepen connections, creating meaningful bonds with others.

4. **Resilience and Adaptability:**

   - Love-based living enables flexibility, optimism, and strength in the face of challenges.

5. **Personal Growth:**

    ◦ Love nurtures self-reflection and continuous improvement, fostering spiritual and emotional evolution.

Call to Action:

"Reboot, Upgrade, Optimize!"

- **Reboot** your mind and heart to prioritize love, kindness, and compassion.
- **Upgrade** your relationships and interactions to reflect the beauty of love.
- **Optimize** your life for joy, purpose, and inner fulfillment.

Experience HALOH – Transform Your Operating System, Transform Your Life!

PAVILION 2

"The Twin Energy-Couples: Generating Perpetual Positivity"

Experience the power of joy through **"Give Joy - Get Joy,"** creating a ripple of connection and harmony, and **"Create Joy - Rejoice Always,"** igniting an inner source of boundless happiness. Together, these principles form **perpetual energy cycles** that transform lives, relationships, and the world with positivity and peace.

Core Concept:

"Perpetual Positive Energy Generators"
The Twin Energy-Couples exemplify the principles of **resonance and amplification**, creating a self-sustaining cycle of joy and connection that transforms individuals, relationships, and communities.

Exhibition Panel Highlights:

Exhibit Panel 1: Give Joy - Get Joy

- Harness the power of reciprocity: giving joy creates a ripple effect, fostering connection and a harmonious exchange of positive energy.

Exhibit Panel 2: Create Joy - Rejoice Always

- Master the art of internal joy generation: by choosing to rejoice in every moment, we become resilient sources of positivity, radiating happiness irrespective of external conditions.

Call to Action:

"Embrace the Cycle of Joy!"

- Activate these **energy couples** in your life to foster inner peace, nurture meaningful connections, and spread positivity to the world.
- Together, let's amplify the energy of joy!

PAVILION 3

Double Portion Projects: Redeeming Lives, Restoring Hope

From saving children conceived in tragedy to providing safe havens for war-traumatized families and empowering the homeless, these initiatives transform despair into joy and vulnerability into strength. Together, we create sanctuaries of healing, compassion, and second chances.

Call to Action:

"Redemption Through Compassion"
Be part of the **Double Portion Projects** and join the mission to save, heal, and empower lives. Together, we can create sanctuaries of hope and build brighter futures for those in need.

Exhibition Panel Highlights

Exhibit Panel 1: Redemption Children Home
"A Second Chance at Life and Love"

- **Focus:** Saving children conceived through tragic circumstances, such as rape, by offering safe havens for mothers and adoption opportunities for their babies.

- **Impact:** Transforming lives by fostering joy and providing a new beginning for both children and their adoptive families.

Exhibit Panel 2: Homes for War-Traumatized Children and Families "Sanctuaries of Healing for War-Torn Lives"

- **Focus:** Providing safe spaces for children and families affected by conflict in regions like Gaza, Lebanon, and Ukraine.
- **Impact:** Helping children heal from war-zone trauma and grow in peace, ensuring a future of compassion and resilience.

Exhibit Panel 3: Redeeming the Homeless "Turning Homelessness into Hopefulness"

- **Focus:** Restoring dignity and providing supportive communities for the homeless through Redemption Community Centres.
- **Impact:** Empowering individuals with resources, work opportunities, and pathways to sustainable living.

PAVILION 4

"Civic Services Innovation: A Blueprint for Thriving Communities"

The **Civic Services Innovation initiative** represents a transformative approach to addressing societal challenges through joy, resilience, and community empowerment. By combining innovative strategies with practical action, these projects aim to inspire individuals, strengthen communities, and create a harmonious and sustainable future.

Strategic Impact:

1. **Health and Well-Being:**

   - Promotes resilience and positivity to improve individual and societal health.

2. **Sustainability:**

   ○ Encourages responsible consumption and proactive environmental care for long-term benefits.

3. **Community Empowerment:**

   ○ Builds strong, inclusive networks that foster joy and mutual support.

4. **Optimized Problem-Solving:**

   ○ Inspires a shift from overwhelming challenges to perceiving opportunities, driving personal and communal growth.

Exhibition Panel Highlights

Exhibit Panel 1: Joy Shield – Building Resilience Through Positivity

- **Focus:** Protecting individuals from negative energy, a root cause of many non-communicable diseases, thus fostering mental well-being.
- **Impact:** Enhanced mental fortitude, joy-filled mindsets, and improved health and well-being, overcoming societal pressures.

Exhibit Panel 2: Posterity Joy Consciousness – Joyful Sustainability

- **Focus:** Tackling climate change by encouraging responsible consumption and sustainability awareness.
- **Impact:** Inspires environmental stewardship and collective consciousness to ensure a joyful legacy for future generations.

Exhibit Panel 3: Joy Circles – Grassroots Empowerment Through Community

- **Focus:** Small groups using the sociocracy model to foster inclusivity, mutual support, and collective joy.

- **Impact:** Strengthens social bonds and creates widespread ripples of happiness and cohesion at the grassroots level.

Exhibit Panel 4: Joypreneuring – Transforming Challenges into Opportunities

- **Focus:** Encouraging an entrepreneurial mindset infused with the positivity of joy to tackle life's obstacles.
- **Impact:** Aligns personal growth with societal benefit, fostering resilience, optimism, and proactive problem-solving.

Call to Action:

"Transformative Civic Responsibility for a Harmonious Future"
Engage with these transformative initiatives to create thriving communities built on joy, resilience, and mutual support. Together, we can pave the way for a harmonious and sustainable future.

PAVILION 5

Joyist Approach to Transform Lives and Communities for a Harmonious World

Redefine Psychological Operations with proactive positivism, thus empowering global unity and creating sustainable societies worldwide. Inspire peace, compassion, and progress to build a brighter, more inclusive future for all.

Main Concept:

"A Vision for Global Transformation"
Showcasing five groundbreaking initiatives that redefine how communities and nations can collaborate to foster peace, sustainability, and progress. Through innovative strategies, these projects address critical societal challenges, empower individuals, and create a harmonious and joyful world for future generations.

Strategic Impact:

"Driving Global Harmony, Empowerment, and Progress"

1. **Fostering Peace:**
Promote understanding, empathy, forgiveness, and collaboration to resolve conflicts and prevent war.
2. **Empowering Communities:**
Encourage proactive solutions to address societal challenges and uplift lives.
3. **Sustainability:**
Build environmentally and socially sustainable frameworks for future generations.
4. **Transformative Leadership:**
Cultivate change-makers ready to push boundaries and lead efforts toward good and noble deeds.

Exhibition Panel Highlights

Exhibit Panel 1: JoyPsyOp

"Transforming Psychological Operations for Global Harmony"

- **Vision:** Redefining psychological operations through positivity, emotional intelligence, and cultural bridging to prevent and pre-empt conflicts and promote peace.
- **Key Features:** Localized hubs, emotional intelligence training, and innovative, heart-touching, and relevant strategies.
- **Impact:** Enhancing global stability and cooperation while reducing the cost of conflicts.

Exhibit Panel 2: The Joyist Unasked Offering Movement

"Unasked Offering: Transforming Lives and Communities"

- **Concept:** Proactive giving of time, talent, and resources to foster trust, compassion, and systemic change.
- **Guiding Principles:** Selfless offerings, compassionate action, and unity in diversity.

- **Impact:** Empowering communities through unasked offerings, joyful giving, and collective problem-solving to create lasting change.

Exhibit Panel 3: Positive Power Proliferation Platform (4P)

"Leveraging Unity Force for Global Transformation"

- **Unity Force:** Integrating military capabilities into humanitarian efforts, including disaster relief and civic development.
- **Positive Power Platform:** Empowering communities through education, skill-building, and environmental stewardship.
- **Global Collaboration:** Partnering with pacifist nations to exemplify peace-driven innovation and sustainable progress.

Exhibit Panel 4: The Joy Dome – Flotilla of Joy

"Sailing for Learning, Harmony, and Hope"

- **Vision:** Bringing hope, harmony, and happiness to the Mediterranean and other volatile/vulnerable regions in the world through DEI practice, peace-building, joypreneuring, cultural exchange, and youth empowerment for excellence.
- **Diploma at Sea:** Training future leaders in peace-building and joypreneuring with practical, real-world projects.
- **Outreach:** Creative merchandise and inspiring messages to engage the public and amplify the mission.

Exhibit Panel 5: Joy Cities

"Clean, Green, Safe, Healthy, and Happy Urban Living"

- **Challenges Addressed:** Crime, hygiene, and sustainability in modern urban spaces.
- **Vision for Joy Cities:** Safe, sustainable, and compassionate environments where well-being flourishes.
- **Impact:** Transforming cities into vibrant havens of happiness and holistic progress for all residents.

Call to Action:

"Empower Global Unity and Transform Communities"
Join the Joyist movement to foster harmony, sustainability, and transformative leadership worldwide. Together, let's create a brighter, more compassionate, and joyful future for generations to come.

PAVILION 6

Caption:

"Joyist International Organizations (JIO): Liberating Systems, Transforming Futures"
From harnessing nature for health and repurposing weapons for growth to revolutionizing education and addressing climate change, the Joyist International Organizations (JIO) lead a global mission to empower communities, foster harmony, and create a sustainable, equitable future for all—starting from the grassroots level.

Main Concept:

"Joyist International Organizations (JIO)"
A pioneering initiative dedicated to addressing systemic challenges and fostering positive change across six critical sectors: healthcare, military-industrial practices, climate change, violence reduction, good governance, and education. By combining innovation, compassion, and proactive action, JIO empowers communities and inspires collective progress for a more equitable and sustainable world.

Key Features:

1. **Healthcare Transformation:** Advocating for a shift from profit-driven pharmaceutical practices to natural, sustainable health solutions.
2. **Peace-Building Initiatives:** Redirecting military-industrial resources toward humanitarian and civic infrastructure development.
3. **Climate Action:** Implementing innovative strategies such as carbon capture and utilization technologies and promoting environmental consciousness for a sustainable future.
4. **Armament Economy Reduction:** Repurposing the Military-Industrial Complex into High-Tech Climate Combat Equipment and Planet Protection Technologies.

5. **Ethical Governance:** Empowering youth at the grassroots with Joyist Circle movements to build transparency, accountability, and ethical leadership.
6. **Educational Reform:** Revolutionizing education with holistic, inclusive, and future-ready programs that prioritize socio-civic and practical skills.

Strategic Impact:

"Driving Systemic Change for a Sustainable Future"

- **Empowered Communities:** Mobilizing individuals and organizations to take action against systemic oppression and promote equity.
- **Sustainability:** Addressing environmental, social, and economic challenges with innovative, scalable solutions.
- **Global Unity:** Bridging divides and fostering collaboration across nations to create a harmonious and inclusive future.
- **Transformational Leadership:** Cultivating ethical leaders and change-makers ready to drive systemic reform and uplift communities.

Exhibition Panel Highlights

JIO Exhibit Panel 1:

"Liberation from the Oppression of Big Pharma Industries: Harnessing Nature for Health and Wellness"

- **Focus:** Shift Big Pharma's shareholder priorities toward natural remedies, nutraceuticals, and functional foods derived from plants and herbs.
- **Impact:** Promote sustainability and public health by leveraging plant-based pharmaceuticals and environmentally friendly practices.
- **Vision:** A healthier world through therapeutic natural solutions that prioritize people over profit.

JIO Exhibit Panel 2:

"Liberation from the Oppression of the Military-Industrial Complex: Transforming Arms to Actions for Harmony"

- **Focus:** Repurpose shareholder funds from militarization to design, develop, and deploy Climate Change Combating Equipment.
- **Impact:** Foster a culture of peace and collaboration, focusing on protecting our fragile planet.
- **Vision:** A unified world built on 'livingry' products, shared prosperity, and collective well-being.

JIO Exhibit Panel 3:

"Liberation from the Oppression of Climate Change Crisis: Creating a Sustainable Environment for Generations to Come"

- **Focus:** Carbon Capture and Utilization Organization and the Individual Carbon Footprint Card to empower youth to consume consciously and have a low or negative carbon footprint.
- **Impact:** Promote Posterity Joy Consciousness, encouraging stewardship for future generations to enjoy the planet as we do.
- **Vision:** A collaborative effort to mitigate climate change through innovation, responsibility, and collective global action.

JIO Exhibit Panel 4:

"Liberation from the Oppression of Gun and Billhook Violence: From Weapons to Tools of Growth"

- **Focus:** Imbibing the belief that only those with the Moral Courage of Meekness shall inherit the earth, not the violent and belligerent.
- **Impact:** Build community capacity for non-violent conflict resolution through education and advocacy.

- **Vision:** A violence-free world where tools of destruction are transformed into instruments of growth and development.

JIO Exhibit Panel 5:

"Liberation from the Oppression of Governance Degeneracy: Empowering Ethical Leadership and Accountability"

- **Focus:** Joyist Grassroots Excellence to educate youth and promote Joyist Circles for grassroots good governance.
- **Impact:** Mobilize communities to promote fairness, accountability, and ethical leadership.
- **Vision:** A brighter future driven by empowered individuals and equitable systems of participative grassroots governance.

JIO Exhibit Panel 6:

"Liberation from the Oppression of Myopic Education: Revolutionizing Education for a Thriving Future"

- **Focus:** Holistic learning that nurtures intellectual, emotional, and social development. Socio-civic soft skills for sustainable development and global citizenship. Neighborhood academies offering accessible and inclusive education.
- **Impact:** Empower lifelong learners with a civic entrepreneurial focus, ready to tackle present and future challenges.
- **Vision:** A transformative educational system fostering holistic growth, relevance, and inclusivity with an entrepreneurial spirit.

Call to Action:

"Transform Systems, Empower Communities, Liberate Futures!"
Drive positive global change through innovative solutions, collective action, and a shared vision for a harmonious, sustainable, and resilient world.

The Standing Ovation

As the **MAGGA Exposition Tour** concluded, the room erupted in a **thunderous standing ovation**, reverberating with hope and inspiration. Attendees marveled at the **visionary ideas presented**, their hearts ignited by the promise of a **brighter future**. Team members and well-wishers engaged in **animated conversations**, brainstorming ways to **transform these bold concepts into reality**. Journalists scribbled furiously, their curiosity piqued by the **audacity and scope** of the **MAGGA initiative**.

For **Yaseva**, this was not the culmination but the **dawn of an era**. The launch of MAGGA marked the **beginning of a divine mission** to align America—and the world—with **God's eternal principles of love, peace, compassion, and joy**. The vision of MAGGA shone as a **radiant beacon of hope**, illuminating the path toward **unity and transformation**.

Together with **leaders, descendants of Abraham**, and **allies worldwide**, MAGGA stood poised to usher in a **new epoch**—

- **Not defined by division, but by love;**
- **Not marked by despair, but by joy;**
- **Not driven by human ambition, but by God's ultimate glory.**

"Make America Great and God Aligned" became the **resounding clarion call**—echoed not just across the Earth, but **heard in the Heavens above**.

A Night to Remember

The unveiling of MAGGA was nothing short of spectacular. The virtual experience was not merely an exposition; it was a **living vision** brought to life through innovation, faith, and teamwork. Each pavilion offered a unique perspective on how **God-aligned principles** could transform every facet of American life—**from governance and education to health, industry, and community well-being.**

The audience was spellbound, their hearts moved by the sheer scope and depth of the initiative. For **Yaseva,** this was a moment of profound fulfillment. MAGGA was no longer just a vision; it was a **living, breathing movement** poised to **change the world.**

The night ended with a **resounding applause** that echoed the collective hope and determination in the room. MAGGA had been unveiled—not just as a concept but as a **beacon of hope** for America and the world. **The stars of Abraham, shining brightly in the heavens, seemed to smile upon this monumental moment.**